Ersatz News

'IT LIVES UP TO ITS NAME'

By Joel Robbins

& Mason Robbins

Ersatz News

By Joel Robbins

& Mason Robbins

No portion of this publication may be reproduced, stored in any electric system, or transmitted in any form or by any means, electronic, mechanical, photocopy, recording or otherwise, without the written permission of the publisher.

ISBN-13: 978-1517399221
ISBN-10: 151739922X
Copyright 2015-17
Joel H Robbins

Publisher
Robbins Books
Nokomis, Florida 43275

THANKS

Where would any satirist be without these masters?

Get your facts first, then you can distort them as you please.
--Mark Twain

Logic: The art of thinking and reasoning in strict accordance with the limitations and incapacities of the human misunderstanding.
--Ambrose Bierce

Democracy is the art and science of running the circus from the monkey cage.
--H. L. Mencken

A gentleman is one who never hurts anyone's feelings unintentionally.
--Oscar Wilde

Nothing is so hard for those who abound in riches as to conceive how others can be in want.
--Jonathan Swift

ACKNOLEDGEMENTS

We're not self-made. We come into the world with an infinite amount of handicaps and privileges. I have to thank my parents, C. M. and Bertha Robbins, my brothers, Terence and Jon, my grandfathers, Werner Johnson and James Robbins who contributed to my welfare. I never knew a grandmother, but they had to affect my personality too; I just don't know as much about how.

Of course my wife Sara, intelligent, talented and wise, plus my children Kristin and Mason, continue to inspire and challenge my opinions. A religious upbringing along with good friends also has to be mentioned.

Jackson Central High School (Arcadia, Indiana), Ball State University, Indiana/Purdue Fort Wayne University, Indiana University and the University of Virginia are credited for my formal education.

These combined to make me realize that all of us are prejudiced throughout our lives and that by personal curiosity, extensive travel, living among other cultures, reading voraciously and broadly, studying at universities we can attempt to reduce some of our bigotry and thereby lower our cruelty to races, religions, creeds, cultures and other socio-economic subsets not our own. I won the economic, democratic, social and educational "lottery," so to speak, yet my formal and informal education has made me conscious of the billions of my fellow humans who still have not won anything but a miserable and nearly hopeless life.

I hope my spoken and written opinions reflect a positive attitude about my relationship to the world, with the hope that my actions backup what I've given lip service to.

--JHR

ERSATZ NEWS

Ersatz News, Views, Sports and Finance--honest, reliable, trusted, balanced, valid, true, unbiased, genuine, dependable, unadulterated, actual, fair, undeniable, unimpeachable, authentic, indisputable, irrefutable, incontrovertible, fabricated satire.

How do you know? We told you! In fact, you just read it here.

Casino Hates Gambling

ERSATZ News—Las Nevada—'it lives up to its name'
O'Haran's Casino and Nightclub escorted patrons from its premises and locked its doors early last Saturday. Despite Saturday being the club's biggest money-making night each week, no gamblers were on its floors after 11:15 pm.

As it turns out, the reason was the gamblers were winning, and, according to an employee who wants to remain anonymous, "Casino's don't gamble, patrons take all the risks."

She went on to say: "We post payouts on the electronic board over the entrance as high as $175,000 on an average night, which really impresses our customers, but most of those payouts go right back into the till through continued gambling at slot machines, blackjack, roulette and craps. Only the casino wins."

The casino's "take" from each game is tracked and automatically reported. Saturday it showed that the casino was down more than $25,000 with no letup in sight, so owners and managers opted to close the casino and investigate. Casino games have a built-in winning margin for the house from 1 to 35 percent. There are no games where the club actually gambles on winning in the long run.

Patrons who were going to walk away from a casino ahead for the first time in their lives were outraged that the owners didn't want to gamble with their own money.

Bill Franklin, who was playing blackjack that night at O'Haran's, said, "I'd be better off playing a game of poker at home with friends where everyone is gambling. I can't believe that if we start to win, the casino stops playing. They don't want us to stop when they're winning."

History Teacher Refuses to Teach Anti-Bullying Curriculum

Ersatz News—'it lives up to its name' – Oklahoma

Since bullying in school hallways, on the internet, on playgrounds, on school busses, during sports practices, on the internet and while walking to and from school had become epidemic years ago, educators decided to take steps to improve the situation.

Plus parents demanded that most school systems take action to end the practice, which, to many junior and early high school students, is just one of those "fun" activities inherent in putting hundreds of children in close proximity with a small number of adults to supervise.

Washington High School initiated an anti-bullying program seven years ago. Principal Sandra Cole says that it has worked well, reducing the number of bullying reports by students, bus drivers, teachers and parents.

But one school employee, history teacher Harold Canter, has refused to promote the program that all teachers were asked to teach and follow in their classrooms.

"Well, I don't like to see students tormented or beaten, but, honestly, to teach anti-bullying alongside an honest portrayal of American history is ludicrous, says Canter."

"How did America acquire the land from the Atlantic to the Pacific? It bullied the Native Americans until they ended up in wastelands. It bullied Spain, England, France and Mexico off their territories. Talk about Jewish, Armenian and other examples of genocide; we did a pretty good job of killing off Native Americans," continued Cantor.

When asked about America today, Cantor responded: "America has troops in 150 countries. Navy ships sit off many countries' coastlines. We've been at constant war since WW II—Korea, Vietnam, Grenada, Haiti, Kosovo, Libya, Iraq, Afghanistan, Yemen, and many others. Name any other country that is as bellicose as America. We have more nuclear weapons that any other country. We spend more on our military than China, Russia, France, Great Britain and five other countries combined. Teddy Roosevelt's Bull Moose Party and attitude fairly represent America's foreign policy—use military threats and sanctions to bully your way to success.

"Why do other countries call us imperialists or hegemons? What would we think if other countries had bases on our soil or flew drones over our sovereign territory to assassinate their enemies?" questioned Cantor. "Also, how has America been able to have approximately five percent of the world's population while using almost 25% of its natural resources?"

Concerning domestic economics, Cantor added, "How does Wall Street work? Bull market? Hostile takeovers. Attempts to work around antitrust laws, big box stores pushing thousands of small stores out of business. How can I teach anti-bullying with a straight face?

"Some educators refer to athletics in schools as 'co-curricular' activities, putting them on par with science, math, language arts and history. Really! The goal of athletics is to physically and psychologically dominate an opponent. Cheers are led and crowds are encouraged to yell, use noise makers and wave posters to intimidate a school's opponent. Do the coaches teach anti-bullying? No! Then why should I?" concluded Cantor.

Principal Cole states that she disagrees with Cantor's philosophy and believes anti-bullying programs are required. She says she will take up his case with the school board, and that that was as much as she could legally say about a personnel situation.

Cantor's response: "I guess they'll threaten and bully me by telling me I may lose my job if I don't become a revisionist history teacher and scrub away or play down America's past and current actions. I doubt they will see the irony of that, though."

JAMES GOLDMAN

The Book of Mormon Revisited

Ersatz News and Reviews—'living up to its name'

How does one describe the Tony-dominating musical The Book of Mormon: vulgar, insightful, bigoted, sacrilegious, disrespectful, satirical, entertaining, iconoclastic, cruel, funny, disturbing—sound like typical American coastal art?

Trey Parker and Matt Stone, the creators of South Park, an animated TV series, pulled out all the stops in their treatment of Mormons in The Book of Mormon.

Hundreds of thousands have attended the musical since its debut in 2010. They probably were not surprised that it received 14 Tony nominations and won 9.

That's because this shocking musical with its catchy songs and exciting and humorous choreography has no down moments, according to many critics.

The oft repeated lyrics, "F--- you, god," probably shocked some, but not any crowd that regularly attends Hollywood produced movies, in which *the F word* gets movies a PG13 rating and a host of additional potential viewers who refuse to lower themselves to view anything with a G.

Fans of South Park also would not be shocked because Parker and Stone make fun of everything and everyone.

After a matinee in Tampa, audience members varied in their opinion of Parker and Stone's work. One said, "It was hilarious. Everyone laughed a lot. I see why it's been so successful."

"When do people normally stop bullying the sweet-faced, kind-hearted weakling? Seventh grade? Then the people who produced Mormon must be junior high students," said one young lady.

A gray-haired gentleman stated: "I liked it. It hit the mark in portraying those religious fanatics, pie-in-the-sky evangelists and dogmatic churches."

"Well, the play pretty well defeated the 'straw man,' now I'd like to see them take on a strong religious opponent, such as the Jews, Muslims, Catholics or Methodists," was the comment of one man.

A gentleman standing nearby added, "I hope Stone and Parker don't take on the Muslims. Look what happened when a few Muslims considered a French cartoonist's portrayal of the Prophet Mohamad in bad taste."

A middle-aged lady said, "Well, it obviously wasn't PG. I was a little ashamed that I laughed at the crude jokes and antics. Feces, dirty words and sexual parts were the source of a lot of the humor. It reminded me of the things we giggled about in elementary school."

"They're (the producers) jerks. It's easier to destroy goodwill than create it. Money and fame and a reputation for being clever at someone else's expense are what they want. Maybe someone will treat them in a very cruel public way just as they treated the Mormons," says one man. "Why pick on people trying to make the world a better place!"

"I was sitting behind several busloads of senior citizens, who were apparently reveling in being shocked by the exaggerated dildos and the mock sexual intercourse taking place on stage. You don't need to quote me on that," said a nicely dressed young lady.

Whether people hate it or love it, performances are sold out, and Stone and Parker now have their place in Broadway musical history.

Royale Caribbeanus to Open Private Resort in Haïti to Local Schools and Orphanages

ERSATRZNEWS 'living up to its name': Labadee, Haiti

Carole Goldstein, President and CEO Royale Caribbeanus Cruises, today announced that RCC will be opening its exclusive cruise stop in Labadee, Haiti, to Haitian schools and orphanages wanting to take field trips. The luxury resort, since its lease to Royale Caribbeanus in 1984, has been strictly off limits to the Haitian public while rich and mostly Caucasian tourists have long enjoyed the jet skiing, parasailing, and surf and sand in the tropical paradise.

"Royale Caribbeanus, after fielding a request from a Returned Peace Corps Volunteer, realized that the exclusive use of Haitian land by penurious foreigners was unjust. We want Haitian children to experience a taste of the opulence we lavish on our customers," proclaimed Ms. Goldstein.

Starting in January, Royale Caribbeanus will begin using buses that are typically used for transporting its low-paid (less than $10 a day) Haitian employees to and from the town center to bus school kids from surrounding public schools and orphanages to the resort. The children will enjoy zip-lining, swimming, massages and gourmet local fare.

-- Mason W. Robbins, RPCV, Reporting from Venice

Television Journalists Protest Beauty Requirements

Ersatz News Bureau: Las Vega—'living up to its name'

More than 25 female television journalists picketed the front entrance to Millionaire Casino yesterday to protest physical attractiveness as a criteria for landing an anchor or reporter position on television stations around the nation.

Millionaire Casino is hosting the biennial conference of professional television anchors and reporters. One protestor suggested we look at all the on-screen personalities on many television news channels. Some have become celebrities in their own right, which often leads to them having to look like movie stars. She added that looks have nothing to do with the depth of their knowledge, media ethics, logic and interviewing skills, yet viewers may respect the anchors' opinions about the news just because they're good looking and speak well.

"The girls are beautiful. Even the representatives of political parties, corporations or charities that are interviewed on news programs are capable of being in beauty pageants," stated Georgiana Wells of Seattle, who holds a degree in broadcast media.

Next to her in the picket line was Tanta Johnson, who added, "Yeah. And while the male anchors have on suits that cover them from neck to shoe, the female co-anchors are showing bare arms, bare necks and their legs to above the knees. What's that all about? What's important, brains or body?"

"Did you notice anything when the attendees entered the casino? It looked like the red carpet for a movie premier. A parade of beautiful people," commented April Long, a young lady looking for a job in television.

Miss Wells continued to explain that she was at the top of her graduating class in journalism, but she is having trouble finding a job. "I'm not fat, but I've always been above average in weight. I don't have as pretty a face as Katie Couric, but I know my business. I'm only offered jobs behind the scenes, while the cuties, even less experienced, get air time."

Signs read: "Grades Not Legs," "Brains Over Bodies," "News Is Not a Beauty Contest," "Male Anchors Should Wear Shorts," "Down with Hems and Up with Necklines," "Hire Brains not Barbies," and "Goodbye Beauty, Hello IQs."

"I can't even get a job as a PR person for a major corporation because they always end up choosing the most beautiful applicant. After the interviews and final selections, I follow up on the Internet to see who they have chosen. It's criminal. It's physical discrimination," complained Hannah Goldberg. "I suppose if I had rhinoplasty, breast enhancement and other plastic surgery I would be qualified to appear on camera. We all should be ashamed."

Religion:
Three-for-One Sale

ERSATZ News and Times—'living up to its name'

The sign in front of the Welden, Nebraska, Holiness Gospel Church, read: "Join Us. We Have the Real Truth." The next week it read: "Three-for-One Sale: Father, Son and Holy Ghost." The other five churches in Welden didn't respond formally, but the local paper, *Welden Weekly*, was swamped with letters to the editor.

"God's not for sale. To sell something, you have to own it. Nobody owns God," wrote Sally Jenkins.

"If Holiness Gospel has the truth? What do the rest of our churches have? The lie?" added Max Lawson, in another letter to the editor.

Nancy Falon wrote, "I take offense to the Holiness Gospel sign that made claims that they are the 'Full-Gospel Church.' What does that make my church, First Methodist? Are we preaching the one-quarter gospel or the one-half gospel? 'Pride goeth before a fall.'"

"I think it's funny that these Christians are arguing about who owns God. God's original favorite was obviously the tiny Jewish tribe. The Jews, Muslims, Catholics and Christians worship the same God, but they all claim that the God of their religion is different and the true God. With that kind of logic, can any religion attract intelligent believers?" submitted Johnny Smith.

According to the Welden Weekly, Holiness Gospel continues to change its sign each Saturday. With the controversy about Holiness Gospel's signs getting play in state-wide newspapers, the Welden Weekly received another letter after the posting of the latest sign: "God only wrote one book. Shouldn't you read it?"

The letter from Akmed Hussein read: "One fourth of the world's population is Muslim, and their holy book is the Quran, which is a direct recitation from God to Mohammed. Get out of Welden once in a while and discover the rest of the world."

Concerning the signs, Reverend Sandy Godfrey, pastor of the Holiness Gospel Church, was quoted as saying, "We are what we are because God is what he is and the truth is truth."

The Days of the Week Are Getting Shorter

Ersatz News: New York—'living up to its name'

Stanton-Walker Publishing has decided to no longer spell out the names of the days. They say by doing that they will save barrels of ink printing their newspapers, magazines and books.

Jeffery Stanton, president and CEO of Stanton-Walker, explained that the days of the week in his publications will now be Mon, Tues, Wednes, Thurs, Frid, Satur and Sund. "Not all languages, Spanish for example, use the word day in the names of their days."

When contacted about whether it might use the same policy. Westingville Publishing House President John Jacobson said, "We haven't really thought about it. It makes sense, though. We don't say Januarymonth or Junemonth. "Jacobson went on to note that we no longer use "third hour" or "fifth hour of the day."

Finally he pointed out that even "o'clock," which was shortened from "of the clock," is being omitted and people simply say, "See you at three."

How did day names originate? A call to the research department of the Jackson Branch of the New York libraries resulted in this response: "My quick answer is that the names basically mean sun day, moon day, Twy's day, Woden's day, Thor's day, Frigg's day and Saturn's day, borrowed from Nordic gods."

"The older version, basically was like what Spanish speaking people use today: Domingo, lunes, martes, miercoles, jueves, viernes and sabado. These mean lord's, moon, Mars, Mercury, Jupiter, Venus and Sabbath."

High NFL Draft Pick Refuses to Sign

Ersatz World Sports—Andarsen, Ohio

Sources from the world of professional football said a top player has refused to sign his five-year eight million dollar contract with the drafting team.

An anonymous executive with the unnamed team said negotiations continue, but no settlement is in sight.

She went on to report that the draft pick had asked during negotiations what local nurses, teachers and social workers' starting salaries were. When he found out they ranged from 40 to 60 thousand dollars a year, he said he would sign for twice that much, or about 120 thousand dollars a year.

The executive added that the player said it would be obscene for a 23 year old to earn millions of dollars playing a game while teachers and nurses earned 60 thousand.

He also pointed out that pro athletes often received a free education from grade school through college, where their athletic skills were also developed at the expense of state funding to a university or fellow students who pay their own tuition and event tickets. "Maybe they should be paying some of that money back just like many graduates have to pay off student loans."

The player says that the short playing and earning days of a pro athlete should be no excuse, because most have college degrees in some field that could earn them a livelihood after sports. "Everyone else has to work for 40 plus years, why not them."

The team reportedly doesn't know what to do with the counter offer, fearing that there will be a backlash from other players if they offer a salary less than a million.

The next offer from the team could be one million dollar for one year, suggesting that the player can give all the money he wants to charity.

An agreement seems unlikely, though, say friends of the player. One related that the player doesn't believe rock stars, movie stars and professional athletes should earn any more than a well-paid professional.

The player has been known to comment that excessive salaries, royalties and celebrity just create people with drug and sex addictions. Television sports, news and reality shows are proof of this.

Possible Five-Dollar Gas Prompts President to Call for Mass Transit

Ersatz World News—Washington.—'living up to its name'

Predictions of five-dollar gas prices prompt the federal government to begin encouraging the auto industry to switch from making cars to manufacturing light rail, busses and other mass transit.

Industry Global Tech News director Jaques Touline says, "Cars have been obsolete for 50 years, but America's love of the automobile has remained. Most of that is because of advertising that sells cars the way you sell new clothing styles."

"Models with a little more or less chrome, different paint colors, a boxier or more aerodynamic look, or other superficial yearly changes have lured consumers into buying new cars just to look stylish. What's under the hood hasn't changed as much as the exteriors since fins graced American cars in the sixties."

US Senator Barry Langlan Callahand said that a bill will start through the Senate soon that will help auto makers retool for the coming changes. Gas prices and proposed federal automobile taxes will make owning a car in every major metropolitan area very expensive. The taxes will be used to restore an economy based on mass transit instead of automobiles and oil.

Rural areas and sparsely populated states, such as Idaho, Montana, Alaska, Utah and Nevada, will be exempt from the federal automobile tax until mass transit can be developed adequately for them.

The Eastern half of the US will have to adjust earlier, but most of these states had mass transit in the early part of last century in the form of interurban rail lines and bus service up until the 1960s. Rails-to-trails bike and walking paths will most likely be converted back to commuter or cargo train corridors between small towns and major transportation hubs. Most people in places like New York City do not own cars now anyway, so many city dwellers will not notice much difference in their lifestyles.

Callahand said, "We can't continue to use oil and gasoline at the current rate. Americans use four times as much as most people in Europe. Plus drivers in Europe have been paying twice as much for gasoline as Americans for fifty years. The average EU driver uses his car only for long trips."

Most families in the world do not own a car or even a motorcycle. That is hard for most people in industrialized nations to believe.

"To get to work they walk, ride bicycles or ride mass transit. There's a tendency to live close to your work so that commuting time is short. "

Driver licenses in most European countries are only available to people 18 or older, and it often costs a couple of thousand dollars to qualify for a license. That means students do not own cars or drive to school.

Touline stated, "Global warming has become a big issue, so millions of Americans driving individually should morally be a thing of the past. Why do people need to travel with a one- or two-ton piece of machinery to simply go to the grocery for a pound loaf of bread and a gallon of milk?"

Ian Witinson, the director of European Multi-Transit Options, a London-based think tank, says, "Americans have been spoiled for years with artificially low petrol prices and freeway taxes. Now they're going to have to live and consume oil products like the rest of us."

Callahand added, "We know the public is going to complain. Citizens every year ask for the federal government to provide more and more services—free health care, schooling, breakfasts and lunches for school children, unemployment checks, housing subsidies, Medicare, Social Security, Medicaid, higher education loans, police protection, etc.—but they don't want to pay for them through higher taxes."

"We have to be realistic. Services cost money. The government can't continue to provide millions of people free services. They're going to have to pay for them the way their parents, grandparents and those before them did. Gas prices have never been high enough to pay for road construction, highway repairs and the massive pollution cars and oil drilling cause."

We see former auto workers joining the job force again making the trains, light rail and busses instead of individual cars.

Since automobiles are the second most expensive budget item for most families and cars depreciate thousands of dollars every year, we see most families increasing their discretionary income by thousands of dollars as they switch to mass transit.

"It's a win-win solution for curbing global warming and replacing lost auto industry jobs while saving families money," commented Callahand.

Clubs Look for Loopholes

Ersatz News: Bartlin, Utah—'living up to its name'

Ersatz News and Views has discovered clandestine clubs sprouting up all over the country—even in small towns. Most cities and towns boast Lions, Kiwanis, Rotary and other clubs, but these new clubs aren't altruistic.

The organizations have different names, but the one in Bartlin, Utah, is called Millstone. Members wouldn't talk to this reporter, but members' friends spoke on condition of anonymity.

The philosophy of the clubs is to pay as few taxes as possible. Besides looking for loopholes, they are hiring tax specialists to assist them in avoiding paying taxes they rightfully owe the government.

The idea for the clubs came from the advertisements on television that target people who owe more than 10,000 dollars' worth of taxes. The ads suggest that the company's lawyers and tax specialists will help them avoid paying some of what they owe. Since then, members of these groups have intentionally fallen behind on their taxes and then sought help from lawyers to cut them in half.

One Bartlin resident, Edgar Hull, commented: "These people are no more than thieves. They complain that the roads and bridges need repair, America needs a strong military, the police and fire departments are understaffed and education needs reformed, but they don't want to pay the taxes for change. If these people don't pay their share, the rest of us e to pay for them."

Beth Downs, a spokesperson for the conservative organization, Fair Internal Taxation (FIT), stated, "These clubs are obviously not made up of patriots. If they were, they'd want to pay their fair share to keep America strong. We have enough lost income from people who hire attorneys to help them receive disabilities or other welfare services when they are healthy enough to earn their own living. Plus, there are lots of other quasi-legal ways to avoid taxes."

She went on to add, "FIT did a study of teachers, for example, that showed many of them cheated the government out of income taxes by accepting cash for the part-time work they did during summer breaks from school. The cash was never declared as income; therefore, it was never taxed."

"We all know the government is mismanaged and there's corruption, but using that as an excuse not to pay taxes is bogus," said Hull. "If there's corruption and wasting of federal funds, vote elected officials out of office. Being corrupt yourself is no way to fight corruption in others."

Downs concluded, "One reason the federal debt is so high is that people want something for nothing. Just think how much money would be in the treasury if we got rid of corporate tax attorneys who are paid huge salaries to discover loopholes in the tax code."

She added, "The government determines how much they need in taxes to make its budget, then businesses find every way they can to make the government go broke. Capitalism only works if there's a strong political and economic infrastructure. Who provides that for businesses? The very government they don't want to support."

US Rescinds Claim to Small Island Off of Haïti

ERSATZNEWS *January 21, 2014—'living up to its name'*

Monday, the US congress voted to repeal the Guano Islands Act of 1856. The Guano Islands Act allowed Navassa Island off the coast of Haïti to be claimed as a US unorganized unincorporated territory. The US claim by an American sea captain came 56 years after Haïti had claimed sovereignty over the island in 1801.

"I think this is an important step in recognizing the legitimacy and importance of Haïti in the history of the western hemisphere and in the present," stated Congressman Richard Burr from North Carolina. "The US really had no right in making claims of ownership of the island given Haïti's previous claim and the island's proximity to Haïti."

Navassa Island is uninhabited and has no source of fresh water. It is currently a national wildlife refuge under the supervision of the US Fish and Wildlife Service. The island was previously used as a source of guano which was mined and shipped to Baltimore to be used as fertilizer in local fields. The miners, all black, worked and slept in slave-like conditions.

The US move to rescind its claim to Navassa was largely viewed as symbolic given that island has little strategic or economic value.

"We see this as a "growing up" of the US government and shows they are beginning to respect the rights of even small countries," stated Haïtian President Michel Martelly. "

I think I speak for the Haïtian people when I say thank you to the US for finally recognizing our legitimate claim to Navassa Island. We will continue to protect the island as the US has as a wildlife refuge," President Martelly added.

The US also stated that it would also compensate Haïti for the value of the guano that was removed back in the 1800's, estimated to be $14 million US dollars in today's currency.

--Mason W. Robbins, staff writer
Location: Navassa Island

Be a Sport

Go-Faster Stripes

Do They Really Work on a Little Miata?
Dan Daniels, Ersatz Humor Columnist

I've done some heavy research on the Internet, and we know how accurate that is just from the memes we've seen posted on Facebook.

Anyway, there's a lot of controversy about sports car enhancements and the level of improved performance they supply. My wife won't let me put racing strips on our Liquid Silver Miata because she thinks it will make it go too fast for safety. I really believe she thinks it will make my foot heavier as I go into a "Walter Mitty" daydream, floor it and careen down the road. I still Google for auto vinyl striping ads when my wife is out of the room, and, when out of the house, flyinmiata.com/V8/.

One sticker I've seen applied to the nicely curved rump of a Miata reads: "Topless is better." This actually slows down a car, at least the passing car with a male driver as he rubbernecks with ogling in mind.

Hang It from Your Mirror

If you're driving too aggressively, even a Phi Beta Kappa key with tassel hanging from your rearview mirror won't convince anyone you're not an idiot. On the other hand, furry pink dice will prove you are.

A club member's "zoom-zoom" reminder stuck to the dash has proven to enhance the sound of the Miata's dual exhaust. Drivers, heeding the message, sit at stoplights pushing down and letting up on the accelerator with a smile on their faces. They believe the more the muffler gets worn the sweeter the sound.

A racing stripe down the length of a car improves the wind resistance about .0002 mph. But if it's a red on white or white
on black combination it increases to .00025. The fact that they're called go-faster stripes proves they make the car go faster, otherwise they would call them car tattoos or something. This is known as circular reasoning which gives extra credibility to my point.

Embrace the Placebo Effect

The greatest benefit of any stripe, swoosh or flame job is the placebo effect. Somehow the carburetor, tachometer and pistons know when the Miata's dressed to race. The result has to be 10 to 20 added horsepower. And if one stripe is good, the second gives an extra boost. It's like red Miata owner Rob Kelt told me: "The doctor prescribed a placebo for my shoulder pain and the pills worked for about 6 months. When I went back she said what I needed now was an extra-strength placebo. The new pills have been working great." So will your second racing stripe. If you want the most benefit, though, slap on a number in a circle. That creates a super-strength, 24-month placebo effect.

If your Miata isn't black, paint one or two wide ebon stripes down the hood, over the roof and over the trunk. As everyone knows, black absorbs heat and heat rises, taking a load off the car, making it lighter and obviously faster. Gray- and white-colored cars reflect light and the downward—opposite and equal—force makes them stick to the road and handle better on curves.

'LITTLE MONSTER'

When I was a kid it was the fad to add mud flaps to a tricycle, bicycle, motorcycle, car or truck.

We jokingly called them "go-faster flaps," because, unlike the go-faster stripes, we knew vertical flaps had to create wind resistance and slow the vehicle. If the flaps on a Miata have a cute saying on them, a company logo, a cartoon cowboy drawing six-shooters or a naked girl, it increases their drag. Sorry for the bad news, fellows!

New wheels, rims or spinning hubcaps don't increase the speed of your Miata, but they do enhance the envy in sports car owners without them. Forget adding horizontal grille bars, as I did, because nobody has even noticed. Bummer.

Giant decals across the top of the Miata windshield can have the aforementioned placebo effect, especially if they read:

"LITTLE MONSTER,"

"MOVE OVER IDIOT➔,"

"MAZDASPEED."

An airbrushed devil's pitchfork, skull, bodice-ripper image, bloody knives or a vampire anywhere on your Miata will get you noticed by the Goth set and wary side glances from middle-aged drivers. Applying stick-figures of a mommy, daddy, three children, a dog and a cat on your Miata back window won't make you go faster, but you'll gain hug points from the ladies. What more can you want!

Sources

"The Miata Fact Book" by Ben Lion

"Miata Autocross" by Otto Speedmore

"Racing Rims" by I. M. Khool

"Pin Striping and Racing Stripes" by Woody Gophaster

"On the Race Circuit" by Holden Sherwin

"Boost Your Miata" by Mark Mieword

"Miata V8 Conversions" by Will Sizemadder

Entrepreneur reveals secret to marketing almost anything

ERSATZ NEWS and VIEWS--Michiana

With multitudes of people watching reruns of Shark Tank and Shark Tank knockoffs, people are clamoring for the secrets of creating a unique product and turning it in to a multi-million-dollar deal. After all, most of the stars of Shark Tank were one product wonders, going from slogging along as wannabees to millionaire status with one lucky lucrative buyout of their invention, app or idea.

"It's simple," says billionaire Josh Mock, obviously not his real name. "Use advertising galore to make people think of and treat your product like a piece of clothing."

That's it? "Yes," he says, "That's it. The consumers are like stupid lumps of clay. Advertising will mold them into whatever you can get them to believe," joshes Josh. "

She, oops, yes, she, says that people are ridiculous about clothes. You can talk them into buying and wearing clothes by the season even in Florida, where it is hot year round. She continued that you can convince them that they won't be considered smart if they don't discard last year's $250 coat for what is in style the next winter. And, you can substitute coat for bikini and winter for summer and have the same results."

When asked if she was insulting the American consumer, she responded, "Of course. If you ask them about their clothing choices, they'll tell you they dress according to their own personality. Sure! All they have to do is look around at their friends to see that they are slaves of the current trends, because people are afraid not to be following the herd."

But, what actually is the secret of "clothing" marketing. "Well," went on Josh. "Change colors, shapes, anything to make last season's style obsolete. You know, planned obsolescence that was the buzzword a half century ago. Oh, how soon we make them forget when it's an insult. What did H.L. Mencken say, "Nobody ever went broke underestimating the intelligence of the American public."

"Take something as mundane as taffy, for example. Fifty years ago taffy was a candy and a color, tan. People named thousands of cocker spaniels Taffy. What color is taffy today? What colors are chewing gums today, and what color was chewing gum 50 years ago? What colors and shapes are cereals? Tennis shoes? Cars? You see?"

When asked for other keys to "clothing" success, Josh replied, "The idea that a product is clothing will lead to other products. A car is a tool, but people deck them out with all kinds of fancy luxuries, which in the clothing industry we would call accessories. These trinkets do not assist the car in getting from point A to point B faster, cheaper or better. They're just fluff. Expensive fluff. Would you tie a red ribbon on your hammer to make it cuter?"

"Notice that owners of cars, which, again, remember are basically tools, feel compelled to wash, wax, polish and even spend hundreds of dollar detailing them. Tools are supposed to work for you, not you for them. We haven't quite gotten the hammer, saw and other tools to this level of importance of color, style, cleaning, maintenance and replacement yet, but, if you go to the big box lumber companies, you'll see we've gotten a good start."

"I've seen people replace an excellent, better made refrigerator for a new, less dependable one just because the color had gone out of style—beige for tan or white to stainless. The same applies to stoves, dishwashers, washers and dryers. We've brainwashed people into believing that style is as important as quality and more important than family economics. Whole kitchens and bathrooms are replaced because of 'style,' whatever that means, and is created by those who want you to buy a new product. Global warming and ecology go out the window when we want people to buy an appliance and toss into the landfill 200 pounds of good, working machinery."

"Lord, the cell phone business is one of the best examples of silliness that an entrepreneur can take advantage of. Pouches, colored protectors, lanyards, and, especially a lot of useless apps that people will pay to put on their phone, tablet or laptop and never use. We entrepreneurs love it. It's like inventing facial tissue. Use and throw away, plus make people pay more if it's colored or moisturized or in a modern looking cardboard box. Facial tissue is for blowing your nose. It's in a cardboard box. We love what idiots people are. They refuse to carry a hankie. It's how we make millions."

Make School 24/7

Ersatz News and Views—'We live up to our name'

It's hard to think of any major facility in any community that is more underutilized than a school. Classrooms are empty two weeks at Christmas, all weekends, a week in the spring and a couple of months in the summer. Plus, most classrooms are only occupied 7 hours a day. I don't seriously believe that school should run 24/7 but maybe 14/6.

Schools used to run from 8 a.m. to 3 p.m. to roughly coincide with parents' daily work hours. Students got out of school late in May and started early in September because farm work used to require a lot of manual labor during the growing season.

Today, many factories run 24/6 or 7 and some major businesses are also open 24 hours a day. Why not have school days and hours reflect that!

Many students, teachers and administrators would be happy to start school at 7 and be done at 3, and others would be delighted to come in at 1 p.m. and leave at 9 p.m. That would address the morning-person and night-person phenomenon. Plus, just think how that would make room for more singletons, advanced or specialized classes that are only taught once a day but are often dropped because of student scheduling conflicts.

Expanded summer schools or a year-round school calendar would also help take advantage of empty classrooms. If school facilities were better utilized, buildings could be smaller, and the tax bill could be reduced. Businesses would have access to teen laborers during the day.

Another bus run might be necessary, as is sometimes set up so that athletes have a ride home after practices, but most of early and late classes could be available only to students who could provide their own transportation.

Haitian Experts Deployed to the United States to Teach Sustainability

by Mason Robbins, staff writer for The Friends of Haiti Times via Ersatz News-- Weekend Edition, Port-au-Prince, Haiti

Responding to a quest from the United States, the government of Haiti will deploy 50,000 Haitian sustainability experts to American suburbs on Friday, one expert for every three suburbs. The experts, selected from remote Haitian agricultural villages, will teach Americans how to live more sustainably. Each sustainability expert will live with an American host family while setting up community activist groups and teaching workshops in sustainability including the production of organic, non-genetically-modified food and humanely killed livestock.

"These are the elite of the elite," quipped Senator Jean Visses Serrier of the Grand'Anse department. "The Sustainability Experts have spent a lifetime honing their skills to exist with very little access to clean water, electricity, environmental control systems for their houses or imported food. They do not receive agricultural subsidies nor can they take advantage of countries with weaker trade protection systems - because frankly they aren't any," Senator Jacques added.

The Sustainability Experts will spend a voluntary service of two years in the suburb to which they are assigned. To begin, the experts will spend 10 weeks in training. The Suburbanites will teach the experts how to speak and write English, forget how to walk, learn to commute long distances in excessively large cars, operate energy-intensive modern appliances and eat out at fast food restaurants. Afterwards, the experts will begin living on their own and begin their work on teaching sustainability.

"The experts understand they will face, at times, extreme hardship. Lack of exercise, inhalation of noxious automobile exhaust fumes and intake of highly processed and engineered food will render some experts too sick to continue their service. In addition, they understand that they are taking a big risk coming here - unlike Haiti, there is a high rate of gun-related homicide. They know the risks that they are taking. Those that can adapt to the largely unsustainable lifestyle of Americans will have their work cut out for them in transforming the suburbs into sustainable communities," a representative of the Haitian Sustainability Corps stated.

While Haiti has suffered from large-scale deforestation, soil erosion and lack of clean water supplies in many of its communities, its people are survivors. Communities have banded together to ensure that they have adequate resources to sustain tight-knit communities which rely on little or no foreign imports. Haiti has used mostly locally-harvested trees for producing dried wood and charcoal to cook food and warm their kitchens. The vast majority of food consumed in Haitian communities is grown locally in the community. Almost all travel is by foot, allowing Haitians to exercise without an electrically-powered treadmill and even say hello to their neighbors. The US on the other hand, has for years relied on foreign imports of oil, food and other household goods while struggling with increasing rates of obesity and related chronic diseases. In addition, America is shifting to natural gas over time but still requires continual importation of oil. What would happen to America's sustainability if the supply stopped?

Of course, the use of these fossil fuels is unsustainable -- here is where the sustainability experts come in.
The discord that has resulted from the unsustainable lifestyle Americans have created for themselves is at its boiling point. The American people have long resorted to imperialistic political policies in order to secure the resources they desire to continue on their current path.

They've obviously had enough and desperately want our help in changing how they live day-to-day," Marie Elnante Thomas, a Sustainability Expert-in-training stated.

Nathan Robinson, a host family father, expressed enthusiasm for the program, "We're all very excited but we know it will be a challenge. We've never bathed less than 15 minutes in a hot shower, bathing with two gallons of cold rainwater in a bucket sounds challenging. We've also never walked the half mile to the grocery store, I guess we'll just take several breaks along the way when we get tired."

Robinson signed up to host a Sustainability Expert after learning about some of the beneficial effects they would have on his community. "I'm particularly excited about their proposal to reduce the use of motorized lawn and garden equipment. Only when the temperature is between 70 and 75 does my family go outside and it seems like everyone else is outside at the same time using motorized lawn equipment. Leaf blowers, mowers, edgers, trimmers...It's so loud outside in the neighborhood we can't even hold a conversation."

The Haitian government is currently working with other industrialized nations to place more Sustainability Experts. "China, Japan, Canada and EU countries are currently on the plan for inclusion in this program. These countries have a lot of work to do become more sustainable like us.

But right now, we're really excited just to be in the US; they're the least sustainable."
Article by Mason W. Robbins, Staff

Don't contact your US senator or representative yet. The article above is a satire. I first learned about sustainability as a Peace Corps Volunteer in Haiti from 1999-2001. We volunteers, fresh out of college, were placed in Haitian communities to try to teach Haitians about things like sustainability. The article above is intended to help Americans understand that we do not have all the answers to world problems and taking a paternalistic approach to third world countries is often misguided at best. We Americans tend to forget that countries like Haiti have valuable knowledge and can provide positive examples for how to live.

.EDUCATION REPORT

Schools Not 99 Percent Anything--Faulkner

ERSATZ NEWS, Arcana, Missouri—'living up to its name'

With pressure from federal, state and local governments to improve public education, it is no wonder that school administrators are finding ways to cheat.

When you look for a nation's literacy rate, you will often see that they boast 99%. America claims a 99% literacy rate for citizens over 15 years of age.

Members of Honest Education for Youth (HEY), a teachers organization that promotes more openness in educational funding and data reporting, attests that most of the data prepared by administrators is adjusted or manipulated to make them look good.

HEY President Darius Faulkner says that anyone who has taught high school seniors knows that the functional literacy rate is probably closer to 85%. "Just have students in the lower-level high school classes read aloud three paragraphs and then have them write about what they have read," she challenged.

She added, "You'll hear them stumble through the text and then when you ask them questions or have them write about the text, they can't. They can say most of the words, but they can't utilize what they have read. And, image the reading level of the 10% of students who have dropped out of high school."

With state-mandated tests putting pressure on schools, some administrators decided to spend more time tweaking the data than making educational reform.

"When the state threatens to take over an underachieving school, administrators start grasping at straws," said a teacher in Arcana with more than 20 years teaching experience. "Some students are intellectually incapable of meeting state standards and immigrant children will need years to reach competency levels. Facing impossible state or federal goals, administrators resort to lying."

"Some states have 'dummied-downed' state tests so that fewer students fail, and teachers teach to the test instead of giving students a well-rounded educational experience," stated a retired Missouri administrator who asked to remain anonymous. He said that state politicians will gladly help find ways for administrators to improve educational statistics because they don't want their state to be listed below 25th when states are ranked educationally.

"In our district, if a student misses two days of school in a row without calling us, we remove him from our enrollment. That keeps our attendance figures high, almost 95%. If he eventually drops out, it doesn't decrease our or any school's graduation rate, because he wasn't our student anymore. He just disappeared from local, state and national data. If he comes back, we just reenroll him. Our graduation rate was 91%," continued the anonymous administrator, "when it should have been about 75%."

Faulkner said that lots of school administrators seek accolades for their schools, which not only impress local patrons but look good when they seek a more lucrative position in another school district. "Titles, such as Hi-Achiever School, A-1 School, Honor Role School, All-Star School, Blue Ribbon School, Gold Medal School and Top-Ten School, are almost always based on data supplied by the school administrators to the state or to the agency awarding the title. So a school will pull whatever strings they need to meet the criteria for one of these so-called honors. Honest administrators either try to explain to their patron why they aren't an A-1 School District or start cheating themselves."

"The whole system of awards is a lot like the 'who's who' books for education, business, colleges, secondary schools and so forth. You can tell these publishers whatever you want and they will print it. There's not much background checking to see how the applicant came up with the statistics or other information," stated the anonymous Missouri administrator.

Drug Testing Coming to Music and Movie Industries

Ersatz Entertainment News—Las Nevados

With the recent deaths, arrests and rehab news about several young movie and popular music stars, it is no wonder that the music and movie industries are working on a plan to reduce use and abuse of illicit drugs and alcohol by their performers.

Kayle Williamshire, a lawyer representing both industries, is drafting the documents that will regulate the testing, fines and punishments for using illegal drugs.

Williamshire says that most professional sports and employers in manufacturing industries require their employees to be drug free. Sports even has regular testing to assure that someone is not using drugs to enhance their performance, unfairly competing with other athletes. Even some high schools have random drug testing.

Members of the music and movie industries believe they need the same thing. Those with some music or acting talent should not unfairly enhance their abilities and stamina with drugs to play concerts or entertain the public. Plus, we have to remember that stars' behavior often affects choices made by our teens.

Before a band would come into a city to perform, its members would be drug tested to make sure they were adhering to the industry regulations. Concerts would be canceled if illegal drug use were found. Actors would be periodically tested in order to keep their membership in acting guilds.

Williamshire continued with the following statement: "The music and movie industries care about their people just as much as the sports industry. Helping our talented pool of musicians and actors avoid drug abuse and its consequences is long overdue."

Upon hearing the news, one music lover commented, "What will happen with sex, drugs and rock and roll?" I guess there will still be two out of three.

College Girls to Sue Television Evangelists for Distortion, Fraud

Ersatz News--Las Angelos—'living up to our name'

Three college girls are compiling a list of television evangelists they think should be sued.

"We're fed up with TV preachers laying guilt trips on the elderly, especially lonely widows, so that they will send money to them," says Bethann Baxter, one of the college girls who established WSWD, What Should Widows Do.

The name is a take-off of WWJD, What Would Jesus Do. Baxter, Kasanya Jones, and Mere Douglas say they believe that Jesus wouldn't be soliciting money from lonely women who have fixed incomes.

Douglas adds, "We've done research on the income of the top ten most popular TV evangelists and found some are driving expensive cars, own multi-million-dollar vacation homes, hire family members at exorbitant salaries, own or rent private jets to travel from one event to another and pursue a luxurious lifestyle."

"Meanwhile, many of their contributors have to apply for free meals, can't repair their leaky roofs and don't have money for new shoes," reports Jones. "It's criminal that TV preachers use all kinds of psychological techniques to get their viewers to send them money."

One technique reported on *www.preacherbumps.com* is to say prayers for the viewing audience. The evangelist will act as if God is telling him that someone has back problems, is in agony with pain in her feet, or is suffering from poor vision. Then he will say a prayer as if it were meant for a single viewer. Baxter muses, most people over 65 have all of these complaints. The preachers are just fishing, and they can't miss. They're really fishing for a donation.

We believe there's fraud, misleading advertising, and deceptive and unethical business practices going on. The shows don't even post a disclaimer, such as, 'Not all promises of healing will be successful. Your check will not be cashed until we have a letter from your doctor assuring us that you are cured.'"

The Website went on to mention healings. Audiences watch while people in wheel chairs get up and walk, and the deaf and dumb start hearing and speaking. "You never see a faith healer restore an arm or miraculously heal a person whose head was cut off in an industrial accident. Show us at least the replacement of a torn out fingernail," laughs Baxter. "Anyone can say they were deaf and now they are healed."

Another favorite, the site reports, are pictures of hungry children in the arms of the evangelist. One national investigative report showed that only five percent of donations to a well-known anti-hunger campaign went for food, while the rest went into paying for airtime, building expensive corporate offices and lining the pockets of those running the so-called ministry.

"Gifts" are also a popular motivation for viewers. Some of the rewards for contributing are plaques, CDs, DVDs, statues, certificates, cross necklaces and books. "The more you send in, the bigger the material reward. Most of the rewards are junk," says Jones.

Douglas says, "Prosperity evangelists are shameless. Jesus did not own a house, donkey, plate, spoon or wardrobe. As bad examples of a follower of Jesus, the prosperity ministers spend tens of thousands on clothes and millions on houses and cars.

"The poor widows who send money to these preachers don't get healed or rich. They just become poorer while making the ministers rich. And, as already mentioned, there is no qualification, such as: 'Not everyone will become rich by sending donations to our ministry, therefore, we will not cash your check until you have become prosperous and paid off your mortgage.'"

Baxter, Jones and Douglas plan to find a pro bono lawyer to file a class action suit against some of the worst offenders. Plus they're not against taking donations from fellow students and others who think the TV evangelists are charlatans. They said they will not use any of the money to cover their expenses for managing the charity, but instead use it to defray legal costs.

The three college students already have 125 stories of fraudulent practices from elderly women. They think they will get about 500 before filing a suit.

When asked about those who believe that TV religious shows bring comfort to many, Douglas said, "Sure, there are some good shows, and the lonely get some psychological benefit from the fake promises and feel like they are giving to a worthy cause, but an evangelist's island vacation home is not a worthy cause. The worst of these preachers know they can't deliver on their promises. As I said, 'It's fraud. And fraudulent advertising is illegal.' The lonely would be better served at their local church or community service organization."

Baxter is a sociology major at Georgia East Technical College, Jones is a criminal science major at Barcelona University in Brazil and Douglas is a recent graduate of Bingington University. They met a couple of years ago at a revival in Texas, then kept in touch through Email before deciding to do something about the questionable practices of many television evangelists.

"We three try to follow WWJD, and WSWD is one way to do that," concluded Baxter. "We're trying to throw the money changers out of the temple."

Big Business to Bail out Fed

Ersatz Business News-New Albany—'living up to its name'

Ben Johnston, CEO of Arzatech, is heading up a consortium of big business leaders to bail out the fed.

"Why would capitalists ask the government to create jobs!" exclaimed Johnston.

So far 14 companies have signed on to loosen their purse strings and see that their companies expand and that more workers are hired.

Several large chains have been asked to change their ownership policies to allow for franchises. Johnston stated: "Why should one man or his family who controls a national or international business make billions and hoard it, when so many people need employment and seek to own and run businesses?"

Johnston expressed that a franchise holder would be happy to earn $50,000 or so a year, not millions or billions.

Some critics say it is the government's responsibility to create jobs and maintain a low unemployment rate. Johnston believes "that is nonsense. Government trying to manage employment means big government, and big government means regulations and more national debt."

Many of those who support Johnston's project say that they have seen what happens when the government tries to control everything—one economic disaster after another.

"If American capitalism cannot support America's economy, provide citizens an honest wage and maintain an adequate standard of living then America's form of

Capitalism is a failure. And I don't think it is," concluded Johnston.

Blandolph Trust calls for more fiscal responsibility

Washington: Ersatz News -- 'living up to our name'

Blandolph Trust, a Washington-based think tank, is searching for actuaries they can support as candidates for congress and the presidency.

Todd Hargrove, director of Blandolph Trust, stated, "We, the people, have been letting the two main parties choose candidates for public office from the ranks of Harvard, Yale, Columbia, Stanford and other high-ranking academic universities.

That sounds good on the surface, but the problem is these schools tend to be more theoretical than practical. The proof that these institutions have failed us is in the performance of the government."

"Insurance agencies and their actuaries," continued Hargrove, "can write a policy, calculate annual premiums and guarantee to pay specific benefits. They do this while making lots of money."

"The government, on the other hand, writes 'insurance' policies concerning unemployment, disability and retirement, sets premiums, and goes into the red paying benefits."

Blandolph Trust released a white paper recently that suggested political parties look for leaders that have real-world experience and who show the ability to apply responsible economic policies in a big business.

Also, government agencies should be headed by actuaries from state universities, small private colleges and tech schools. "If insurance companies can stay in the black, then the government should be able to too," concluded Hargrove.

A US Senator who asked to remain anonymous, said, "That's all bologna. The government isn't a business. Its job is to protect and support the citizenry. I think we do a great job of that."

"I don't know who this senator is, but he needs to have a talk with his financial advisor," added Hargrove. "No Edward Jones or Ameriprise agent would agree that you're doing a good job with your personal or company finances if you continually spend more than you take in and borrow money you can never pay back."

US Ceases Recognition of Columbus Day as a National Holiday at the Request of the Haitian Government
Eersatz-au-Prince, Haiti
October 12, 2015

    Last month, the Haitian government asked the United States to cease its celebration of the Columbus Day holiday.

    "Clearly from history, we understand that, in no way, was Christopher Columbus a man to be celebrated," stated Haitian Parliament member, Jean Tholbert Alexi. Monsieur Alexi, standing in the oppressive heat outside the unfinished parliament building, was referring to the rape, torture, enslavement and murder of the Arawak Indians Columbus found on the island of Hispaniola.

    Former US House Member and Returned Peace Corps Volunteer Tomas Todd, added to Alexis's sentiments: "Columbus really had very little influence on the permanent settlement of North America by European invaders." Todd lived and worked as a Peace Corps Volunteer on the Dominican Republic side of Hispaniola. "Saying Columbus discovered America is comparable to saying Icarus led to Neal Armstrong walking on the moon," he mused, "After all, how did he discover it if there were already people living there. Therefore, I hereby announce that Columbus Day is no longer a national holiday in the US."

    While the loss of Columbus Day as a National Holiday will provide one less marketing opportunity for major US corporations, most US citizens will barely notice; most don't have the day off and there are few traditional celebrations tied to the holiday.
--Mason W. Robbins, International Correspondent

Washington—Ersatz News Magazine

Congress Offers Souvenir Bill for National Parks

A bill in the House of Representatives would ban selling foreign products in national park gift shops.

It also could require any business within 10 miles of a park boundary to advertise honestly about the souvenirs they have for sale. Especially if the business is catering to national park visitors

Bill Fredrick, a shop owner outside of Smokey Mountains National Park, asked if he would have to put "Chinese Souvenirs" on his shop sign instead of the current "Cowboy and Indian Shop."

Fredrick went on to say: "Let me be brutally honest. We give our customers what they want, cheap, stamped out, foreign-made products. If we tried to sell handcrafted goods, we'd go out of business. Few American customers appreciate quality. Now, take your foreign traveler, he may look for a quality piece, but not your American."

The committee editing the bill put out a statement that said the bill's intent was to help revamp the image of America's manufacturing ability. Ed Bailey, editor of *Economics Today and Tomorrow*, said, "Millions of foreign travelers visit our national parks each year and apparently go away believing that Americans can only produce junk. Our own citizens look at the labels and think Americans can't even do that, since they don't create the junk that's on sale at or near national parks."

After the committee presents the bill to the House for a vote, the Senate would also have to approve the measure, then it would go to the President for signing.

Congress Passes Term Limits by Narrow Margin

Ersatz World News-Washington

A surprise move on the part of the new wave of senators and representatives brought a term-limit bill to the floors of both houses and it passed.

After the President signs the bill, senators will only be able to serve one six-year term and house representatives two two-year terms.

Plus, past congressmen will be banned from running for the same office again.

Senator Wayne Goldman stated: "This is long overdue. Being a congressman was always meant to be a service, not a life-long career."

Representative Betsy Wells added: "The parties have become so entrenched that those of us coming in with new ideas have trouble voting our conscience or truly representing our district. The ranking members of congress tell freshmen how to vote."

Tom Jones, political talk host on WZED, Omaha, says, "Congressmen are campaigning year round and during their entire terms. Every time you hear one say the words liberal, conservative, Republican or Democrat, they're campaigning for their party and not truly focusing on issues."

"This bill is a step in the right direction," Jones added. "The longer a congressman is in Washington the more he becomes indebted to lobbyists and big businesses that contribute to his reelection campaigns."

The President is scheduled to sign the bill next week sometime.

Defense Department Seeks to Expand Reach

Ersatz Daily News—Washington

The Defense Department proposed last week to expand its influence around the world. The US already has bases or troops in 150 countries, so expanding to cover 180 of the 191 countries of the world would not be difficult.

Obviously, stated a DOF spokesperson who wants to remain anonymous, it would be advantageous to have troops in all countries, but Russia, China;, North Korea and a few others would resist that.

Most countries appreciate America's world-policing policy, and even some don't have standing armies because of America's protective treaties.

The nations who depend on America's superior military might, save billions, or at least millions, of dollars a year by not having to own and maintain an air force, military bases or troops.

Critics of America's foreign police say that the USA is ostensibly a hegemon, which is something most American politicians blame other powerful nations of being.

Adding another 30 countries to the 150 America already helps protect, or bullies, depending on how you look at it, would require a minor increase in the defense budget, claims the DOF spokesperson.

Opponents to this expansion include James Farthing, member of Farthing-Banton Institute, a Washington-based think tank, who claims America needs to bring its troops back home to protect American soil. He states: "Expanding the CIA operations substantially would serve the same purpose as all those bases and troops and would be less costly."

HINDSIGHT

Profane and Vulgar Words

I'm amazed how many words we can't say in adult company. Even people on TV will do a report on race relations and have to use "the N word." Are we children? Are we afraid that some bully maniac will beat us up or kill us if we write or say the real word? I'm sorry to say, yes, that could happen.

Does anyone alive over five not understand and say in their mind the entire N or F word when we say *N word* or *F word*? The same holds true with the written f**k. What do you say in your mind when you read f**k? Fuh asterisk asterisk kuh? No, you think the real word.

If not, then you haven't ridden a school or public bus or walked through a high school hallway. Sometimes when I want to talk about controversial things I feel like a kindergartener learning the alphabet when the letter of the day is Mr. F. "Children, do you know a word that starts with F?"

They're liable to say F**k, because they've heard Mom rip it off while talking on the phone about a SNAFU (look up the origin of this acronym) at her place of business during a supposedly relaxing weekday afternoon, or from Dad when he bumps his head under a sink whiling doing plumbing. Of course if they watch movies, attend sporting events or talk to kids in the neighborhood, they know a good Mr. F word. When a football player fumbles the ball and walks off the field, his favorite word is often you know what.

What I never understood was why so many of the vulgar terms we insult people with are really about women. If we call someone a p*ssy, Bas**rd, or SOB these terms actually reflect on and insult women too. Why attack women in general when our intentions are to put down a specific person, usually a male. Words are symbols, not real things. We have to get over pretending our feeling are material things. All of our parents probably told us something like this when we as children came home crying because someone had called us a name: "Sticks and stones may break your bones but words can never hurt you."

Well, most of us know that we have a tendency to be hurt by epithets even when we know they're wrong. We should practice what we preach.

My Sunday school teacher told us not to use damn, hell and sh*t, and then added that dang or darn, heck and shoot were just words that were substituted for damn, hell and sh*t. God, Christ, Jesus or Jesus Christ became gosh, cripes, jeez or gee whiz or jeez zoo. He told us a substitute for another word still passes on the original word. The real meanings of gosh dang, gosh darn and frig are obvious.

Another question: Why are terms that should refer to loving behavior used in a negative way? Examples: "You're screwed." "F**k you," and "I got the shaft"? Another puzzle is that it's more acceptable to use a profane word on TV than a vulgar word. *Pro* and *fane* mean *for* and *church, temple* or *shrine*. "Oh, my God" and similar phrases should not be used outside that setting, where it's considered offensive or sacrilegious.

--Franchesca Alexandra, Ersatz News Guest Contributor

Women Protest Insults by Skipping TV Advertisements

Chicago Ersatz News—'living up to its name'

Many ads tend to hint that women are ugly, dirty, and stinky. They add to the insults by suggesting they have stringy hair, saggy breasts, misshapen bodies, bad breath, nasty nails, poor complexions and colorless faces. Cosmetic companies gross about 10 billion or more a year by making women feel bad about themselves.

While ads tell them they're fat, they bombard them with advertisements about romantic meals at ethnic restaurants and easy-to-serve, but fattening, take-home food.

To fight back, women are taking a page out of the sixties and trashing their bras. Along with this retro move, one group has decided not to buy eyeliner, lipstick, rouge, powders, hand and face cream, body oils, hair coloring, teeth whiteners, perfumes and cosmetic surgeries for three months.

They're also not buying stylish clothes if they can't afford the items and, instead, spending the money on activities that are really good for them.

They're trying to encourage other women to make it a nation-wide movement. Raechelle Braxton, president of Just Love Us (JLU), gave a list of reasons for this move: "1) Men don't have to spend thousands of dollars a year out of their budgets on cosmetics to attract the opposite sex or to land and hold jobs; 2) It's wrong for women to think that the natural oils in their scalps, hands and bodies are unnatural and must be removed to be replaced by products made from petroleum, vegetable oils or animal-fat products; 3) women should not be judged on how colorfully they have painted around their eyes or on their faces and nails; 4) only in affluent cultures are natural odors considered offensive, requiring masking with animal or artificial scents. I could go on.

"The most embarrassing thing about cosmetic or other ads that focus on the superficial is that women have come to believe that they can cover up poor eating habits and lack of healthy exercise with expensive products. Even worse is when money that could be used for higher education and other résumé-building activities goes down the sink or shower drain every day in the form of perfume, beauty oils, makeup and creams," continued Braxton.

Jon Johnston, exercise physiologist and nutrition specialist from Hampton-Dodge University, agrees with most of what Braxton says: "If women want to have that special sparkle in their eyes, a rosy color in their cheeks and a body that looks good in any type of clothing, they need to eat right, exercise daily, and get outside in the sun a little each week. My studies also show that women who keep up on current events and read books of any kind improve their liberal education and fare better when looking for a long-term relationship."

Jessica Long, a JLU member, added: "I want to be perceived by men and women as intelligent, knowledgeable, competent, healthy and physically attractive, in that order. Therefore stylish clothes and makeup are at the bottom of my list and education, self-improvement, exercise and eating properly are at the top. I think it's ridiculous that women feel like they have to show bare legs, breasts, bare arms and their bellies in public. Can you image a man in Wisconsin on TV every day forecasting the weather in a wife-beater shirt, shorts and sandals? No, he'll wear a suit, and the female weather person next to him will have on a sleeveless dress with a hem above her knees."

"I hate to put it this way, but I have to be honest. If you're fat, out of shape, poorly educated, and unhealthy, all the clothes, colognes and makeup in the world won't solve your problem," commented Raechelle. "I want women to be proud of themselves and make real strides toward cultural equality. They shouldn't let advertising determine how they feel about themselves."

Elle Dawson, who quit the advertising business because it preyed on women's psychological weaknesses, suggests that women tape their favorite TV shows and watch them an hour later, which would allow them to fast forward past the insulting ads. Also, she's not buying women's magazines, which make millions by putting down females for not looking like the airbrushed models on their covers and in their articles.

Dawson added, concerning jewelry ads, "Every kiss does not begin with a necklace or ring. Men shouldn't have to buy affection from their spouses. A kiss should begin with love."

The Hanging Gardens of America

Ersatznews—APIC--Cityscapes

With air pollution from cars, buses, factories and power mowers increasing, cities are begging architects to design buildings with roof gardens.

Aerial views of cities where "hanging gardens" are present show trees, bushes, flowers and vegetable gardens greening the view.

Bethann Saunders lives in a nine-story apartment building that has a 40,000 sq. ft. garden on top.

"My husband and I love taking the elevator up three floors to the roof with a basket of homemade food and a bottle of wine. We have our own building park," brags Saunders. "Tables, chairs, benches and other outside furniture are placed among the trees and flowers for the use of residents."

Some roofs have winding paths lined with flowers, which are maintained by volunteers who like to garden.

"The envy of all of us are the tomatoes, squash and green beans that one neighbor raised in one corner of our roof last year," adds Saunders. "I have a feeling more of us will want to grow tomatoes that can be picked ripe, when the flavor is the best rather than the firm ones at local stores."

City horticulturist Ben Freisen says that the plants will absorb carbon dioxide and give off oxygen that will reduce pollution. He also says that the trees and bushes on roofs will help cool buildings in the summer.

ERSATZ MEDICAL NEWS
Erectile Dysfunction Drugs Popular with Non Sufferers
Kali Wayne, Porta Punta

Sales of ED (erectile dysfunction) medications have skyrocketed in the last couple of years. Pharmaceutical firms are thrilled, but mystified, by the rapid growth in distribution.

Conch Surveys in Key West, Florida, polled two thousand doctors and found something surprising—many who don't suffer from ED have been requesting the three leading prescription medicines. Most doctors won't prescribe the medicine if the patient admits this, but many will.

CSKW interviewed people who were taking the medicine for ED and those who weren't. Billie Wayland says, "I don't have any trouble with ED, but since my wife died I miss sex. Watching the TV ads for Cialis and Viagra and their warnings about sudden decreases in vision, temporary hearing loss, rapid breathing and racing heart, I became interested. Those are the reasons my wife and I made love."

Another man, who called himself Joe, said, "Yes, I take the drug. I don't tell my girlfriend, though, but I'm proud that I can maintain an erection lasting four hours. Wouldn't you be?"

Other men responded in the same way. Unlike most men taking ED medication, who fear side effects, these men talked their physicians into prescribing the drug *for* the side effects.

Stocks and Bonds Today
Ersatz News New York

Wall Street Springs a Leak

It was a leak last year, it is a stream now and it could be a raging river by the end of the year. Investors our streaming out of Wall Street onto main street.

Fed up with brokers and financial investors controlling the nation's economy, smart investors are being their own middle men. Clete Waybirth of Seattle asks, "Why should I hand my money to a financial advisor who hands it to a brokerage firm who puts it in the stock market? My advisor drives a Mercedes and his wife has a BMW convertible. I drive a Honda and my wife has a ten-year-old minivan."

He added, "When my job cut back hours and my wife was laid off during the recession, I had to sell the Honda. My nest egg in stocks was shrinking. Meanwhile, my financial advisor was having an in-ground pool installed, and brokerage firms were giving bonuses."

Investors like Waybirth are looking to main street for sources to loan to directly. They also want more than a piece of paper saying they own a part of a company. Frankie Jon Bedford of Paoli, Ohio, commented: "When banks loan money, they hold your car or house for ransom. When I buy stocks, businesses offer me nothing to protect my money."

Betsie Congland of Newark invested in a friend's local custom window and door factory, and she's happy about it.

Congland said, "The company was having trouble getting a loan from the bank, and I wanted my money out of Wall Street's hands. It was a win-win deal. Plus, the owner offered me collateral in the form of a forklift and a Bobcat.

I'm getting 7.5 percent on my money. Try to get collateral from a company or mutual fund your financial advisor wants you to loan money to."

Bronson Ackluss of Las Mesas, Arizona, wondered: "How did we ever let Wall Street and MBAs run, or after the banking mess should I say ruin, the country? Let's get back control of our own finances."

Haitian Special Forces Recently Took Back Eleven Million from Federal Reserve Bank New York

Ersatz News New York, NY 12/3/2013

On Monday, US government filed a grievance with the United Nations regarding what they termed "looting" of the Federal Reserve Bank of New York by Haitian Special Forces over the Thanksgiving holiday. According to US officials, Haitian Special Forces, in a covert operation, broke into the bank in Manhattan and removed $11 million in gold.

"It's an international outrage", said an angry US official who wanted to remain anonymous because she was not authorized to speak on behalf of the government. "They have no right to enter US territory, let alone steal money from the US people. They will answer for this action."

Apparently, security at the US treasury at the time was lax due to its being a national holiday (one that was made up in 1863 by President Lincoln with no known ties to a Pilgrim-Indian feast). The Department of Homeland Security has already begun an investigation into the matter.

"We have a legitimate right to that gold," stated a representative of the Haitian government who also wanted to remain anonymous because he was not authorized to speak on the matter. "The US marines raided the Haitian treasury in 1914, at the beginning of their two-decade-long illegal occupation of Haiti, stealing $500,000 in gold on behalf of US bankers. New York bankers had loaned the money to the Haitian government at interest rates that could only be considered usury by any reasonable person."

Joseph Theodore, presidential spokesperson, acknowledged that the Haitian government had taken the money back. "The $500,000 stolen in 1914 is the equivalent of $11 million in today's currency. We were not given a fair chance to repay the money and the interest rates of the loans, given Haiti's desperate financial system at the time, were predatory by today's standards and standards then. We intend to repay the $11 million but at reasonable interest rates."

The UN responded to the grievance by asking the US to work out a repayment plan as proposed by Haiti. "$11 million is pennies to the US government. They can afford to loan the money to Haiti, which is working on many critical projects aimed at reconstructing Port-au-Prince following the 2010 earthquake. There are still a lot of people living in tent shelters in the capital almost three years after the earthquake. I'm sure the US wouldn't mind providing this assistance to Haiti in order to rebuild homes for these people. We suggest the US forgive the actions of Haiti and move forward on working out a repayment plan," stated a UN official who was authorized to speak on behalf of the UN but wanted to remain anonymous because he didn't know if he could speak on this issue and feared US reprisal.

"This aggression will not stand, Man", said a US citizen standing on a corner in the US capitol in a tie-dye shirt. "We must take military action and get back that money. I'm afraid I won't get any more food stamps if that money is lost." Asked if he wanted to be quoted for this article, the citizen stated that he did not but didn't know why.

Another US official, who also wanted to remain anonymous because he was not authorized to speak on behalf of the government, stated, "The UN and Haitian proposals are ridiculous. The American people don't care if tens of thousands of Haitians have no homes. We need that money. Every American will have to eat at McDonald's one less time this year if we don't get that money back immediately. This could be a catastrophe!"

The US is expected to respond to the UN and Haitian proposals for the development of a repayment plan in the next week --MWR

Public Shocked as Lawyers Start Suing Lawyers

ERSATZ News—Seattle—'living up to its name'

Insurance company attorneys are beginning to be directed to sue personal-injury lawyers in the state of Washington.

Monroe Insurance President William Hays says, "The personal-injury guys used to be called ambulance chasers. They don't want to be attorneys; they just want to make money."

Research shows that handling personal-injury cases is big business. Television viewers can seldom get through an evening without having to watch two or three industry advertisements.

The June issue of Right Consumer Magazine reports that the main targets of these attorneys are insurance companies, automakers, doctors, and pharmaceutical manufacturers.

In defense of the attorneys, Right Consumer states that the world is much safer because lawsuits force businesses to adhere to higher health and safety standards.

On the other hand, Hays claims, "Some of these personal-injury settlements are ridiculously high, driving up costs that must be passed on to the consumer. The goal of a lawyer is to make money. He won't take the case just to make the world a better place."

Recently, according to Right Consumer, attorneys are now making big money by helping people avoid paying their credit card bills, gain questionable disability compensation or reduce income tax payments they rightfully owe.

The magazine went on to report that the lost revenue, which runs into the billions, resulting from these actions obviously have to be made up by those who pay their bills and taxes honestly.

Another problem, mentioned Hays, is the "Feds letting upper level management at auto companies and banks run their companies into the red, bailing them out, paying off the rich and giving nothing to the shareholders, some losing thousands of dollars invested for retirement. Why don't these 'kind' lawyers go after that money that was bilked out of the wallets of the middleclass?"

Hays concluded by saying: "There are lots of good, honest lawyers, but the ones who are hurting America are the ones who don't follow the intent of the law, rather they try to find ways for people to not have to obey laws. We're trying to take these guys to court themselves."

Road Work All Gummed Up

ENN & Ersatz News—Acadia, Florida

Littering laws just got more complicated in Acadia, Florida, according to its mayor, Bailey Johns.

"Yes, you heard it right, we're encouraging people to throw their chewing gum on our streets," says Johns.

According to town board member Latisha Appleton, informal studies by Acadia's street department workers show that dark gum spots are found on most of the town's sidewalks: "It appears to wear better than the concrete, so why not use it to coat our streets."

"We're not too crazy about sticky gum that can be transferred from the sidewalk to shoes to store carpets and tile, so we're asking people to throw their used gum onto the streets," states Appleton.

Johns added that he hopes the discarded gum will cover the streets and reduced asphalt repairs and maintenance costs.

When asked about littering and gum sticking to things other than the road, he says "the gum usually gets pressed firmly to the pavement then gets a layer of dust after it's been run over a few times. It stops being sticky."

"Concerning littering, we have never actually ticketed anyone, though maybe we should have, for spitting out their gum on sidewalks, but now we encourage tossing it onto our streets," says Johns.

Turn On, Tune In, Drop Out

Ersatz News-Sacramento

An old saying just got a new meaning. The drug message of the past has been transformed from "turn on, tune in, drop out" to "turn on, plug in, drop out" and other variations.

Now two of the leading tablet, cellphone and video-game companies have devised chips that can be implanted permanently in both the optic and audio nerves. So, get ready for "plant in, turn on, drop out."

That means no more having to carry around a device—everything will be invisible to others and controlled completely by speaking or blinking.

The ADDA is excited about how these implants will help the handicapped. Doctors will benefit financially because they will have to perform the implanting.

Educators and parents, on the other hand, are worried. West Washington principal Cal Wallens says, "It's already hard to keep students from using their cellphones, hand-held video games and IPods during classes. Now it will be impossible."

Belle Thomas, a mother of three, says she will not allow her children to get implants: "They already spend too much time fiddling around on Facebook, Instagram, Google, Twitter and online games. I see parents pulling microphone buds out of their children's ears now so that they will listen to them. Plus, how do you know the kids won't stay up all night surfing the Web."

Hakim Ammahit, who has four children, complains that when he travels with his children he continually has to confiscate A-V that they smuggle into the car. "If I don't do that, they never look out of the windows, and, when we stop at an historical sites or geographical wonders, they don't want to get out of the car."

Employers are concerned too. One stated that when he peeks over the top of cubicles in his offices now he sees people playing solitaire, engaged in war games and watching porn. Being directly wired, he said, would make it impossible to catch them, get them back to work or fire them.

Wyandotte County May Crack Down on High Decibel Mufflers

By Carol Jones, Ersatz News—'living up to its name'

"I live near the interstate and the noises from the traffic are annoying. There's a law against semi air breaks in the city limits, but I wish there was a ban on warn-out mufflers in the county," says Jim Cowand.

Cowand hasn't been the only one concerned. Hundreds of calls and emails have streamed into the county commissioners' office. Ersatz News tagged along with Tomas Golar, a county commissioner, as he used a decibel meter to check the sound levels of the vehicles traveling along State Highway 89, one of the busiest near Fairplay.

His notes showed that a couple of brands of American motorcycles were the worst offenders. Ironically enough, the least noise came from European and Asian motorcycles. Old trucks and cars with obviously warn out mufflers came in second behind the American motorcycles.

Golar says he doesn't know what to do with the information he gathered with the decibel meter, since some of the motorcycles were new. He added that he assumed that they were loud not because the mufflers were bad but because they were either "poorly designed or intentionally loud."

Fellow county commissioner Jake Tolan and Golar discussed the problem over lunch. "I've had motorcycles for 40 years, and mine never sounded like these new ones," claimed Tolan. "It reminds me of a Briggs and Stratton 3.5 hp lawnmower dad owned back when. Noisy as hell with a tiny muffler. I don't understand why these American motorcycles have to be so loud.

"My motorcycles sounded like finely engineered machines while today some of the motorcycles remind me of the old hit-and-miss engines."

Research shows dB levels increase exponentially. A 10 dB increase pumps the noise level two times. A 70 dB would be 10 times louder than a 60 dB and 100 times louder than a 50 dB. Cars in some states are limited by law to about 70, while some motorcycles hit 100 dB.

State Transportation Director John Zimmer said, "We used to require all vehicles have a periodic safety check, which included measuring the loudness of the car, truck or motorcycle exhaust system. We may have to go back to that. If the manufacturers are intentionally producing noisy mufflers because drivers love, well, uh, you know, to show off, I don't know what we'll do."

Renegade News Group Hounds High-Profile Anchors

ERSATZ NEWS, Basston, Georgia—'living up to our name'

Anchors of major 24-hour television news organizations are getting a taste of their own medicine. And they don't like it.

Renegade News, a group that sends news items to local cable public access channels, decided that they would add a little balance to news reporting.

Reggie Banks, founder of the news agency, said that she was tired of watching people who were involved in tragic situations hounded by news organizations wanting to make money from their tragic story. She related that the news agencies put mobile TV units on the streets where victims' houses are, have reporters calling all day, station reporters on the walkway in front of their houses, push mics and cameras in their faces and chase them down streets.

Banks' group is now doing the same to major anchors of 24-hour news organizations and the major television network news anchors and producers. They have posted people on their sidewalks, interviewed their neighbors, conducted background checks, followed them in cars and called them numerous times during the day asking questions about their personal lives.

Lots of embarrassing personal information has resulted from all this work and Renegade News is happy to broadcast it on public access channels. Banks says that some commercial major channels have contacted her about creating a reality show based on their work.

The anchors, on the other hand, are furious. They don't like the tactics used by Renegade, even though they are the same tactics the major news organizations themselves use every day to pry into victims' lives, emotions and tragedies.

Some of the anchors and producers are attempting to get restraining orders, but Banks says they're going to have to admit that their own actions are illegal: "I'm not worried. I'll just post stories about their attempts to limit freedom of speech or press."

SCIENCE Forum:

New/Old "Green" Breakthrough

Central Columbus Communicator & Ersatz News-'living up to its name'

"It's time for those who treat 'green' as the latest fade to get real," stated Lionel Jackson, professor of bio-agriculture at the university. "Green isn't a style to brag about, discuss over cocktails and pretend to follow."

According to Professor Jackson, the university has completed studies of local suburban landscaping techniques and styles and compared them with several test sites. He said the typical suburban yard is cropped short and requires bag after bag of chemicals to keep it green. The older trees were cut down and few and shorter trees replaced them.

The test plots are allowed to be natural, which Jackson explains means grasses indigenous to central Ohio are allowed to reach their normal height and to reseed automatically. Mature trees are left on the plots. Wildflowers are not dug out or killed, so they add color and variety to the landscape.

"Many people who think they're green, yet spray poisons on their yards to kill dandelions and other native plants that aren't grasses, have a completely false idea about ecosystems," added Wendy Sanders, a colleague of Professor Jackson. "Not only are dandelions beautiful, children love to pick them, blow on their umbrella-like seeds, and people used to bread and fry the flowers or cut the greens for salad."

She suggested that if people Google 'edible dandelions' they will find recipes for a French cream of dandelion soup and also dandelion wine. The site suggested harvesting the leaves before the plants flower; otherwise the dandelion greens will be bitter.

Professor Jackson says he loves to make dandelion wine and uses the leaves in green salads: "But I can't imagine people eating the leaves after they have sprayed poisons on the yard and treated it with four or five other chemicals."

Bill Holbrook, who lives with his wife Jennifer on one of the test plots, said, "It's a little hard to get used to. Neighbors that build the old way don't like the looks of our yard. We only mow enough space for our kids' outdoor games that require short grass. The rest is as nature intended."

"The people on both sides of us want their yards to look like their living rooms, so they want only one kind of grass and they want it buzzed so it looks like a short-shag carpet," said Jennifer. "They sometimes ask me how I can stand all the shade from the large trees, so I tell them we love to sit under them and feel the cool breeze."

"Our neighbors don't use their mown yards or sit under trees. If they go outside they complain about how hot it is and run back to their air conditioned family room," mentioned Bill. "Some won't let their kids dig mud holes in the yard, make bases for softball, or ride their bikes through it. It's no wonder kids sit in their rooms all day in front of an electronic screen of some kind."

Professor Jackson's studies showed that the test plots absorbed eleven times as much carbon dioxide as the typical suburban yard and gave off three times as much oxygen. He added that another plus is the decreased use of electricity to run A/C in the summer because the houses and, especially, the windows are shaded by leaves, and the trees direct higher, cooler air down around the house to make a refreshing current.

No poisons are sprayed or applied to the yards, so there is no need for tiny signs saying to keep off the yard or don't walk in the yard barefooted. "The test plot owners saved lots of money and were far more green than neighbors who were still treating their property in the old-fashioned way," said Professor Jackson.

Jennifer said that she wished she lived in a green community because she hates sitting outside under a tree with her family having a picnic or just talking while the neighbors are mowing, trimming, sawing, and spraying, which all are done with loud motorized tools blowing blue or black smoke or noxious fumes and poisons. "I don't think they mind the noise other neighbors make because they don't go outside. But when we're outside sometimes we have to stop talking until the riding mowers stop, or go inside when we smell that they're spraying poisons. We use a push mower and hand clippers for the little section we mow."

"I know people who won't use a Styrofoam cup but mow an acre of lawn and broadcast bag after bag of fertilizer and poison on it," laughed Professor Jackson. "They don't want anything about their yard to be natural."

First-Person Report

Americans Lose Weight and Gain Health in Haïti

M. W. Robbins, ERSATZNEEWS Reporter

Day after day, at the international airport in Port-au-Prince, droves of pudgy Americans are waddling to taxis bound for the countryside of Haiti. Their mission: To lose weight quickly through lifestyle modification.

"We Americans have for a long time admired the slim and trim physiques of the Haitian people. Now, Americans have the chance to model the Haitian lifestyle to improve their health and lose weight," said Ettice Courtney, Hope for Americans in-country program director.

So how does the program work? "Hope for Americans partners with members of rural Haitian communities to find host families for obese Americans. The Americans then pay the host families a reasonable monthly fee to cover the costs of room and board. While living with the host families, the Americans learn the lifestyle of the Haitians by participating in the family's activities of daily living. The weight starts coming off the day the Americans arrive," Ettice continued.

A ride-along visit to a Hope for Americans participant's site clearly demonstrated why the program was so effective in stimulating weight loss. After a 45 minute flight in a vintage Russian-made propeller plane from the capital, I was greeted in the provincial capital of Jeremie by a current participant, Joe. A solid, athletic man of 45, Joe smiled broadly as we shook hands. "You ready for this?" said Joe as he squeezed out of a wry smile. "Let's eat first," Joe said, and started off down the dusty street in a short-sleeve button-down shirt, shorts, sandals and a straw hat.

From the airline's office where I had been dropped after the flight, we walked 10 minutes to a local restaurant. After a meal of rice and beans and Creole chicken washed down with soda pop from glass bottles, we began the hike to Joe's site. After two and a half hours and 15 kilometers of walking on mountainous dirt roads and goat trails, we arrived at Joe's host family's house. After meeting the family, it was off to the chores. Joe and I spent the remainder of the afternoon fetching the day's water supply, smashing peanuts in a large mortar and pestle to make peanut butter and retrieving the goats from a remote family field. Joe has lost 75 pounds over five months living this way. He says he doesn't even have to watch what he eats.

"Joe's results are pretty typical of people who have tried our program. Participation in the rural Haitian lifestyle just melts the fat away," Ettice proudly stated after my ride-along-visit.

Hope for Americans' goal is aimed at encouraging American participants to return home and continue the lifestyle changes. Joe echoed this hope while sharing his plans for returning to America. "When I get back to the States, I'm selling my car, riding lawnmower, edger, blower, trimmer and chainsaw. I realize, now, these powered devices eliminated the activity I needed in daily life to be healthy. And maybe my neighbors will now be able to hear some of the sounds of nature since I won't be blaring engine noise from my backyard every weekend."

Given the success and popularity of the program in Haiti, Hope for Americans is looking to expand to other countries around the world.

Let's See the Light

Ersatznews: Fort Wane—'living up to our name'

Astronomers, and yes, maybe astrologers, are loving the new trend in enjoying light from the moon, planets and distance stars.

The cause, according to meteorologist Ken Barnes of KWKW television, is that whole neighborhoods have opted out of having street lights on during portions of the evening and early morning: "People in the city can now see thousands of stars instead of maybe a dozen."

Mayor Ted Johnson believes that "it's a good idea. I know it saves the city thousands of dollars in electricity bills and also means we have to replace bulbs less often."

The big worry by some in the neighborhoods testing the LSTL (Let's See the Light) program is that crime will go up in the darkened sections of town.

The Mayor responded that "although the neighborhoods to be darkened are announced ahead of time, we also remind residents that we will adjust police patrols to give the dark areas more coverage. We also encourage residents around the city to join the Neighborhood Watch program and solicit volunteers to get outside and walk the sidewalk for the several hours the lights are off. If it's a rainy night or completely overcast, we leave the lights burning."

"This must be what it was like when cities were required to have blackouts during WW II," said Sandi Federer of one community recently darkened.

Not only does Barnes announce blackout times and neighborhoods during his evening weather report, he invites people in the darkened communities to meet him at an open park, a football field or an empty parking lots to participate in some star watching and identification.

"I point out Venus, the North Star, the Space Station, and satellites, the Big and Little Dippers and Cygnus the Swan. We often use Google Sky on our cellphones to locate constellations," added Barnes.

Many times an amateur astronomer will bring a telescope and focus on the craters of the Moon or the rings of Saturn.

Mayor Johnson says, "I like seeing Fort Wane citizens walking the streets, greeting their neighbors and enjoying the night sky without ambient light. Like Barnes, I often join one of the starwatching groups to take in meteor showers and other wonders of the sky. And, as a reminder, we haven't seen a rise in crime in these blackout areas. The streetlights go back on during the times we know are the highest in crime."

No term limits for congress on near horizon

Ersatznews and Views—Washington- 'we life up to our name'

Hopes by groups like Honesty in Government and People of Power were dashed this week as a House bill that would have created congressional term limits did not get out of committee.

Most long-time Beltway observers were not surprised. The general consensus is that government hasn't changed for congressmen for a couple hundred years because they make their own rules.

In a rare moment of honesty, a Democratic congressman having a drink at a bar near Capital Hill said, "Term limits. No way. This is the best job possible. You get a free office, financial perks, and women around Washington are throwing themselves at you."

Another congressman at the table added, "Don't mention our names, but, you know, the electorate isn't that smart. As long we pour money into our district by pork-barreling or create more ways for lazy people to earn money without working, we get re-elected."

The first congressman jumped in with "Yeah, we can spend money the nation doesn't have, bomb countries without declaring war, and basically spend our time in Washington partying, and nobody cares. The ones who are complaining, which has been going on for a hundred years, aren't listened to."

The conversation led to all of the unethical and unconstitutional actions that have been committed by politicians without causing the citizens to refuse to re-elect them. One was about the sexual acts between pages, interns and congressmen.

With a lot of laughing going on around the table, one congresswoman even dared to say, "We could probably let you put our names with these stories and still get elected if federal moneys continued to flow to the right people. I have a great job. I don't really have to go to the floor and vote or even be in my office, because most of my constituents don't know what I'm doing. I do have to campaign and also spread a lot of BS around my district."

Honesty in Government spokesperson Blake Fryerston grimaced when told about these comments: "Everyone knows about this corruption and abuse of power. I saw the Maxwell Anderson play, Both Your Houses, the other evening, and I think it was written in 1933. What he attacked then is still going on today in the 21st Century. We get promises without change and accept them election after election. These career politicians are laughing at us, and we're too stupid to curb their greed and hubris."

The Filthy Rich Lack Sharing Spirit—World Wide Study Shows

Hong Kong, Ersatz Chinese Bureau—'living up to its name'

A new study by World Wide Wealth shows that the wealthy of the world don't like to share.

Ben Taylor, executive director of WWW, reports that those making less than $35,000 a year are more likely to give a higher percentage to the poor than someone above that amount.

One reason, states Glenn Williams of Loans for Living, is that "the rich in America, Europe and world capitals don't think of themselves as rich."

"If you have a room in your house for your car, you're rich. If your children have a room of their own instead of having to sleep in the same room as Mom, Dad, Grandmother and siblings, you're rich. If you have electricity and running water 99% of the time, you're rich. If you have a house and a cottage, you're filthy rich," added Williams.

"A billion or so people's daily discretionary money wouldn't buy that Starbucks coffee on your desk," joked Williams.

Taylor commented that one of the first things you learn in kindergarten, besides not pushing and not running with scissors, is sharing what you have. "Many of the obscenely rich have forgotten that lesson. Some say that the poor like being poor. Others say that the poor are poor because they are lazy."

"I try to tell them that if they had been born in a dictatorship, to poor parents, to the same lack of public education, received poor health care, that they would be poor and hoping someone would share with them," continued Taylor.

"If you lived in the heat and humidity of the tropics without air conditioning, only got one minimally nourishing bowl of rice a day, and were suffering with several intestinal parasites, you'd seem lazy too. So, how should the rich help the poor? Studies show that government handouts are more harmful then helpful. "I obviously believe in Loans for Life and other help organizations such as Kiva. We provide money for loans in second- and third-world countries. Big banks won't lower themselves to help these people because they're making big deals with the Fortune 500," says Williams.

Taylor suggests multi-week or longer "mission" trips to help people learn about marketing, saving money and reinvesting. "Too many businesses run by the poor are hand-to-mouth operations, meaning that they spend the gross income without any thought of restocking shelves, medicating their livestock, repairing equipment, etc. The businesses die of mismanagement."

"There's plenty of money and resources for everyone in the world, so it's a shame that some will have a million in the bank, millions in mutual funds, and more millions in property while others in the world scratch in the dirt for pennies and hope someone will share their knowledge and loan them money," stated Williams.

ERSATZ INTERVIEWS

Media Editorialist Loses Ratings by Attacking those Employing Fallacies to Dupe Listeners

Joel Robbins—This is Joel Robbins with the ERSATZ NEWS wakeup show, The Early Bird, broadcast on WRTZT 102 fm. We always live up to our name. I'm here with Frances Watts, host of Watts Up! on NCN Cable News Saturdays at 2 pm. Good morning Fran, how are you?

Fran Watts—Fine. Glad to be on your show.

R—Glad you could be with us. I've read your book, Making Sense. Very good.

W—Thank you.

R--Few people study philosophy and rhetoric, so understanding when a writer or speaker is attempting to change your opinion with faulty logic is hard to determine. For years during your syndicated NCN Radio and Television broadcasts you have listened to politicians, experts, professors and authors support their opinions illogically. Was that the reason you wrote Making Sense?

W—Partially. I didn't want to insult guests by calling out their mistakes, so I ignored them and went on with the interviews. Once or twice when I did note faulty logic, my guests weren't very happy and the interview went downhill from there. Finally I decided that I could initiate a discussion of the problem by writing a few editorials, which ended up being part of my book. I didn't like that the people being interviewed were getting away with debaters' tricks. The interviewees sounded like they had common sense, but did my listeners know they were being manipulated?

R—So you wanted to help your audience.

W—Right! I didn't want my listeners to be swayed by poorly supported opinions on any program but, especially, my program. After all, my viewers often seemed to be tuning in wanting advice on what and who to vote for in upcoming elections. I didn't want to be doing them a disservice."

R—Could you give our listeners an example of faulty logic?

W--Let's say you are a politician. I'm your opponent and have done some research on you and your family. During an interview I am asked about you. I answer: You know, don't you, that Robbins's sister grew up a Muslim, his father belonged to the Masonic Lodge, he served in the Peace Corps not the military, and he, personally, supported socialist Tommy Golf's minimum wage increase bill in the Senate?

R—You really did research me. And those comments sound typical of the kinds used in campaigns.

W--Those statements represent a host of logical fallacies: veiled suspicions, prejudice, red herrings, post hoc ergo propter hoc, fear mongering, composition, division, ad hominem, hasty generalizations, begging the question, and circular reasoning.

R—Let me get out my English and Latin dictionaries.

W—No need. Ignore the names of the fallacies, concentrate on the method used to deliver the attack.

R—I don't understand.

W--Even though my comments could be taken as qualifications you might need to be a politician making good decisions in this diverse century, I would be hoping to hit one of a listener's prejudices.

R—So, make good things look bad!

W-- I heard a politician say that Franklin Delano Roosevelt was a great president and he would have voted prochoice if he were alive today just as all fair-minded people support women's rights. This statement could be attacked for several fallacies. One, 'begging the question,' because F.D.R. was a great president is opinion not a fact, and we can't predict what his opinion on abortion would be. Two, appeal to authority, where the speaker calls on the authority of a famous, but deceased, person to imply that he back would the speaker's opinion. Three, over generalization (the use of *all*) and going along with the crowd. Four, equivocation, meaning there are several ways to define fair-minded but the speaker is using it only to mean his side of the question. Five, either/or, black/white fallacy, ignoring that there are shades of grey between black and white.

R—Whoa! This isn't easy to follow.

W—That's why talking heads with their sound bites get by with it.

R—I've listened to some speakers bombarding the audience with comments like you mention without giving listeners time to think whether they make sense or not. We leave with only the speaker's opinion but not logical understanding. It seems similar to propaganda.

W—Exactly. I watched a debate between talk show hosts Jon Martin and Bill Riley on my computer a year ago and it was sadly disappointing. Martin's a comedian that just overpowers his audience with mugging, logical fallacies, meaningless one-liners, half-truths, and insults that play to the audience. He's a riot but a lightweight when it comes to debating, knowledge and logic. But people take his barrage as truth because it's clever. His lines, though lacking depth or logic, are funny and therefore memorable. Riley also plays to his audience, but, except for a few silly emotional appeals to his fans in the audience, pinned Martin to the wall mercilessly when it came to debating, common sense and depth of knowledge. After the video I read comments from viewers of the video, and two-to-one, they named Martin the winner. That's embarrassing when you understand logic and debating.

R—If the audience is anything like me, they may be struggling to keep up with these new terms, complicated definitions and examples. Could you supply us with a simpler example?

W—OK. This common logical fallacy is called post hoc ergo propter hoc (after this therefor because of this) or (one event causes another). One speaker claimed when President So-in-so and his party took office he caused the unemployment rate to rise, global warming to increase and initiated another war. Obviously one man taking office is only one of an infinite number of events at any moment in time that might cause economic, political and social upheavals.

R—So, it's the blame game without connecting all the logical dots.

W—That's one way to describe it, but advertisers use it in reverse to make us feel that an expensive set of golf clubs will improve our skills, the latest jeans will make our daughter cool or owning 10 acres in the country will lead to security.

R—It's everywhere, and I'm an interviewer too. So, do you have anything else I should look for in my daily work to protect my listeners from those utilizing logical fallacies?

W—One more. An old trick is called a red herring, which means the speaker tries to distract the listeners from the argument at hand. If questions from the audience focus on the discrepancy of the speaker's views on the family, women's issues and his recent divorce, the speaker might say something, such as, you know my opponent smoked marijuana when he was in high school. In other words, if you don't have a good comeback, throw out a red herring and maybe no one will be clever enough to catch that you changed the subject and avoided answering the question. Magicians call it misdirection. They'll say look over there and then take the man's watch.

R—Do you have a special word or two to leave us with?

W--I hope our TV and radio audiences become educated so that they are not susceptible to rhetorical sleight of hand. Googling to find a list of logical fallacies, definitions and examples is a good place to start. Listening to taped TV and radio interviews instead of live ones allows the listener to stop, look up words, check facts, and catch people using logical fallacies.

Stalking, the New Hunting Sport

Kyle Langer, Ersatz Sports—'living up to our name'

Hunting has changed a lot in the past 50 years. Hunters own high powered, long-range rifles with scopes and range finders. A deer, for example, often won't know a hunter is in the area until it finds its rib bones crunching, feels a searing pain, hears the rifle's report and finds it is almost impossible to breathe.

In the past, hunters used to have to spend weeks in the field scouting out deer habitat, hiking for miles, learning tracking techniques and then sneaking up close enough to the animal to make a clean, humane-as-possible kill shot.

Although some sportsmen still hunt this way, many of today's hunters hire guides, drive an ATV to the range, hunt over animal baits or shoot from hundreds of yards away with long-range ammunition.

Now hunters in some western states have initiated the practice of having the hunters being hunted. While in the field, the hunter is being stalked by a pellet-rifle-carrying hunter—called a stalker. Kids have long played war with BB guns, which when shot seldom penetrated the skin through clothing. The stalkers carry a pellet gun that has a maxim soap block penetration of 1 inch at 30 yards.

Tests have shown that there is no penetration when the hunter wears heavy duck pants, but the pellets often draw blood and always leave a bruise.

To maim or kill the deer hunters is not the point, so those with pellet guns are reminded to aim for the thigh. Hunters are not allowed to shoot back, but if they detect a stalker with a pellet gun, they are allowed to call him off. Then the stalker has to retreat and cannot continue the chase for 5 minutes.

Besides that, the animal hunters are only allowed a handgun, bow, crossbow or short-barreled rifle that is accurate to approximately 50 yards. No baiting, guides, scopes or range finders are allowed.

After the hunt the stalker and hunter meet and discuss the adventure.

Lane, another hunter and stalker, commented: "I love the sport. I don't care if I kill an animal, because I have plenty of money to buy meat. Like most hunters, I'm out for the sport. Stalking makes hunting more fun whether you end up with a trophy or not. I just wish it were legal."

Departments of natural resources don't condone the practice and in some states stalking is illegal. Stalkers and hunters have to sign waivers in case of a serious wound or death. After all a hunter might duck suddenly and a pellet that's meant for the thigh might hit him in the head.

Bill, a hunter who participates in stalking and has been shot twice, says: "You can't believe the difference in hunting when you're being stalked. It is more sportsmanlike because it takes some of the modern advantages away from the hunter and gives the animal more of a natural chance to survive. You can't just concentrate on the prey. You have to watch your back."

Sheryl, also a stalking proponent and friend of Bill, adds, "You think your adrenalin is high when sighting in on a deer, well that's nothing compared to having to worry about being shot as you track your game. The prey is also the prey—you have to be on the alert at all times. Your heart beat goes wild and you get this unbelievable rush. Unlike Bill, I haven't been shot yet. My fingers are crossed."

Rice Farming Gone, USAAID Refocuses on Eliminating Corn Farming In Haiti

ERSATZ October 7, 2015: Washingdon

A representative of USAAID announced a new initiative to eliminate corn farming in Haiti today.

"This initiative is very much aligned with our mission statement which is as follows: Our Mission: We partner to end extreme poverty and to promote resilient, democratic societies while advancing our security and prosperity," USAAID spokesperson Mat Herick explained.

In the past, USAAID was successful in virtually quashing rice farming activities in Haiti. USAAID did this by flooding the market with cheap, subsidized US rice during the harvest of local rice. With corn, which is harvested year around in Haiti, the approach will be a bit different. USAAID plans to flood all markets with US-farmed corn continuously until it's evident that no corn farming remains.

"We do not want Haitians providing for themselves; that only promotes security and prosperity in Haiti while doing little for ours. Highly subsidized US farmers need to maintain their mega-farms and all of the equipment required to run them. They can't do that if they don't create dependent people like the Haitians. I mean, that's USAAID's goal, to promote our prosperity," Herick added.

The elimination of corn farming will be modeled after the elimination of rice farming. Here's how it works. The US government buys surplus corn from US farmers. USAAID then places the corn on the market in Haiti at prices which undercut locally-grown corn. Private remittances from Haitian ex-patriots are then used by Haitian citizens to buy the corn. Thus, US citizens buy the corn twice then hand it to Haitians. In this way, all of the US taxpayers' tax dollars, as well as most of their after-tax income sent to relatives in Haiti, is filtered back into the US economy while creating a culture of dependency in Haiti. It's clearly a win-win and aligns perfectly with USAAID's mission.

USAAID plans to report on the outcome of the program in a congressional hearing in one year.

Your Dollars Can be Golden

Jeff Hanibal, Guest Columnist--*Ersatznews*--Seattle

The federal government used to back its currency with gold (called the gold standard), then silver, then, well, paper, which means US currency is backed by nothing. Now, thanks to Gand$ (Gold and Silver Sunset Brokerage), your money can again be gold.

Value can be added to a new credit card from Gand$ using gold or silver. You give a Gand$ broker the precious metal and he will add Gand$ to your card that can be spent just like US Dollars.

The value of a Gand$ card is that in case of an economic crisis the credit on your card is backed by gold (a tangible commodity) and not thin air. Unlike gold that you hide under the bed, lock in a safe or pay someone to safeguard for you, it can be spent any time without any trouble.

All those pre-1965 90% silver quarters people have been hiding in their closets can now be deposited with Gand$.

How does Gand$ make money? They have a one-time startup fee and then take 2 percent on every deposit of gold, which is a handling fee like the credit card companies charge retailers. Those credit card handling fees are approximately 4%, which retailers pass on to the consumer with markups.

So, what happens to the gold when Gand$ gets it? They have to store it for you and relinquish it to you or someone you have given Gand$ to. Until then, it's just like dollars spent on any credit card.

Of course the worth of a Gand$ fluctuates according to the precious metals market. That can be troublesome, but we also know that the spending value of a dollar goes down each year because of inflation.

So, if we earn 5% on a bond, mutual fund or stock investment and inflation is 3%, then our spending money only increased in value 2 dollars on a hundred. Plus the government will take a percentage of your interest in taxes.

Gand$'s President Tony Roberts says that if Gand$ catches on, the company will add other precious metals, such as platinum and palladium, and maybe gems to items that can be deposited.

LOCAL VIEWS

How Corrupt Is your Local Government?

--Sam Grogan, Columnist for Ersatz News

National studies by 50 state universities representing every state show that local governments are more corrupt and incompetent than the federal government.

I know, most of you are questioning how local governments can be as corrupt as the federal government that has a 20,000,000,000,000 dollar debt. So you have a 100,000 dollar annual income. Take that times ten, times ten, times ten, times ten, time ten, times ten, times ten, times ten, times two:

$100,000.00
$1,000,000.00
$10,000,000.00
$100,000,000.00
$1,000,000,000.00
$10,000,000,000.00
$100,000,000,000.00
$1,000,000,000,000.00
$10,000,000,000,000.00
$20,000,000,000,000.00

Pretty scary! Now think of 50 state governments, thousands of county governments, hundreds of city governments and thousands of town governments.

The people who run these entities all have friends, fraternity/sorority brothers/sisters, relatives, a good-ole-boy network and acquaintances. Money isn't just passed under the table.

It's distributed through free country club memberships worth thousands, real estate tips where roads and parks will be built totaling billions, unauthorized use of public vehicles worth millions, jobs to relatives adding up to billions, pay-to-play totaling billions, hundreds of schemes you wouldn't believe if someone told you and other shady transactions.

Probably only one percent of those conducting corrupt deals are ever exposed and face charges, and, as you know, the papers and TV news highlight a new indictment every week.

Who pays for this? You do, unless it's the federal government, and they just print more money to cover their corruption and ineptitude. Local governments also aren't spending their own money, so why should they worry about waste or corruption.

Next time you wonder why your money doesn't go as far as it should, think of the corruption of local government officials.

Get Real
News Dominated by Views

Several of the top cable networks have stopped being primarily news channels and are now focused on views. More viewers are returning to local channels and a couple of foreign news organizations to find out what's really new.

Polls show:

> Who covers straight news the best? Cable—15% Noncable—28% Foreign Cable—57%

Admitted news-junkie Sal Jenkins says, "During the past election, cable news focused on one story and talking heads simply repeated their opinions every day hour after hour *ad nauseam* for 8 months. I switched the channel to find better news coverage."

"They don't give the news, they show up at events, which changes the news," said Tom Zainel, Seattle resident. "People start doing crazy things for the camera, then go home and watch themselves on TV. They should report news, not make news."

"It's ironic that one station was criticizing one candidate for having beautiful women in his office and businesses. This story was delivered for two days by female anchors who were gorgeous. There wasn't one that couldn't have been a beauty queen," laughed Brooklyn Maines. "And they were showing bare arms, necks and thighs while the male anchors had on long pants, shirts with tight collars, sport coats and ties. What hypocrisy!"

Other criticism of cable news channels is that the reporters are made into celebrities. Some believe that they should be behind the news reporting anonymously instead of being stars.

Those reporting on media have called the new journalism the old "yellow journalism." There's the constant out-of-breath claim of BREAKING NEWS even when the story has been reported for days. Every story is hyped. Sadly the camera often zooms in if the persons being interviewed might show they are going to weep.

Others cite the repeated use of "then something went terribly wrong," "appearance of impropriety," "she went missing," crime, trial or game "...of the century" and other phrases represent "purple prose." When the air clears after an incident, viewers realize what they've been watching is really "non news."

Often the number of dead is inflated or a breaking news story has to be retracted after they find the real data or facts.

--Boggs Callahan, Ersatz News Columnist

Citizens Ask: What's in a Name?

Pinepark, California: Ersatz News—'living up to its name'

The crowds are gathering in the downtown around the courthouse of this tiny suburb of Los Angeles. News teams from the USA, Canadian and Europe have vans parked along streets. Gawkers are there for the spectacle. The reason? Not to ogle participants leaving the courtroom after one of the area's thousands of celebrity divorce settlements. It's about creating and passing a law concerning how we name babies officially. No, REALLY!

Pinepark County Council has decided that babies should be named using their mothers' maiden names. In fact, states Glen Miles, a Pinepark attorney, the "term 'maiden name' will soon disappear from local birth records. As soon as we get the laws changed children will always be named for their mothers."

Judge James Satchel, who is not part of any of the petitions involving the "name game," as the initiative is now called, says, "This move makes sense to me. The patronymic naming of babies went out of style in most tribes a century or more ago. You still see the ov and ova in names such as Navratalov or Navratalova, meaning son of or daughter of. The Celts, for example, used son or daughter of John for Johnson or Johnsdattir. Of course, the bin, ibn or ben in the Arab world still means son of. Then you have O and Mac as patronymic prefixes. But in America today, we can now stop the practice completely."

"If you've been in my courtroom during paternity hearings or watch the 'shock jocks' on daytime TV, you'll know how easy it is to verify who the mother of a child is, but to determine the father takes DNA testing," continued Satchel. "With Family and Child Protective Services cases where a child is removed from the home, it's confusing, expensive and time consuming for counselors, law enforcement officers, home inspectors, supervisors, Guardian ad Litems, lawyers and judges to wade through all the nuclear family names and extended family names. Those involved in a case sometimes create flow charts to map out who is related to whom and when and where. Having one consistent name flowing from great grandmother, through grandmother and mother to child would be very helpful."

Tam Samuels, standing outside the Pinepark courtroom, says, "The men hate to admit it, but sometimes we wives stray and bear children by friends and neighbors. We even jest when a family of blondes produces a redhead—'Must have been the milkman,' we joke. In these cases, the state misnames the child after the legal father rather than the biological father."

A *Times City Sentinel* editorial included: "Since land was passed down the male line in Old England, legitimate children were always given the father's last name. Now that anyone can inherit estates, utilization of paternal names is no longer that important.

"Since using the maternal name is highly accurate in correlating the child to the birth mother, and the paternal name, especially in Los Angeles and other big cities, is often faulty, why not choose the former."

"This is all bogus. The town just wants some publicity," read one of the many signs being carried by onlookers. "What do we do with John Smith Jr., the second and the third?'

From comments in the crowd, men are upset because there has been a long tradition of men, in the home, church or government, controlling christenings. Note that the Holy Bible runs Jesus's lineage from Adam through Joseph, even though Joseph is not the biological father.

Sandy Cummins, a mother of four and Pinepark State Bank president, added, "America seems to be behind on lots of issues. Take for example switching to the metric standard, having a female president, abolishing the Electoral College and adopting a phonetic alphabet. Maybe we can at least lead the way on a child naming system that makes sense in a modern world."

HINDSIGHT

Electoral College Soon to Be Eliminated

After studying the last election, the focus, beside two horrendous leading presidential candidates, is: How did the system take the vote away from the electorate?

Well, the most famous way is called the Electoral College. The so-called college is a collection of people who make the final choice for the presidency. You're not voting for a candidate, you're actually voting for someone who you hope will vote for your candidate. Since politicians are afraid you won't vote the way they want you to or you're stupid, this removes you one step from a direct vote. Hillary Clinton won the popular vote and Donald Trump received the most electoral votes, meaning that he became president with fewer of the citizens' votes.

In the primaries, you might have heard of delegates. Again, no matter whether you're voting Republican or Democratic, you aren't voting for a candidate, rather you're voting for someone who is supposed to vote for who you want them to at a party's convention. Step back again.

Step back one more time if you supported Bernie Sanders in the Democratic primaries. Before any debates and platforms were explained, Hillary had about 400 Super Delegates pledged to vote for her at the convention and Bernie had about 50.

Super Delegates are made up of past and present Democratic office holders and Democratic leaders, including Hillary's husband Bill. Obviously the Super Delegates weren't waiting to see how you, the public, voted or what the candidates stood for before pledging. Unlike going to the polls to select a candidate, you didn't have the opportunity to vote for or against these delegates. Plus, most had already decided who the Democratic candidate would be before you even thought about the elections.

I know you don't want to step back another time, but, sorry, you have to. There is also something called a PAC (political action committee). Individuals are limited by how much they can donate to a candidate, which limits their influence over the candidate if elected. People who want to attempt to 'buy' a candidate anyway can use a Super PAC to donate as much as they want. Hillary had millions of dollars in support from a Super PAC; Trump and Sanders had no money from them.

Ad agencies and psychologists are paid big money by both Republicans and Democrats to figure out how to touch your heart strings, ignite your prejudices, arouse fears and schmooze you into believing elected officials will remove corruption from Congress, balance the federal budget and improve your life. Guess what, they haven't done any of those for a 100 years. The psychologists guarantee that their methods will work for their candidate, but they're not sure the psychologists on the other side aren't better at manipulating a voter's psyche.

I won't mention voter fraud, dead people voting, people voting twice, those who sell their vote for a beer, and so forth.

Ok, there's another one. The Democratic National Committee is designed to support Democratic candidates who are running for office--ALL the candidates without preference. In the 2016 election, several members of the DNC resigned because it was discovered that they were working to undermine Bernie Sander's campaign to assure Clinton received the nomination. And you thought you were making a difference with your vote.

Then there is something called the "good ole boy" system which is heavily used in politics. How do elected presidents pay back those who supported them? The answer is: help with highway and Department of Defense contracts and political appointments. How do you think Hillary came to represent the Empire State as a US senator when she was from D.C., Arkansas and Illinois? How did she become Secretary of State? Didn't Democratic and other voters soundly reject her in the 2008 presidential primaries? Right, you guessed it; it's the good ole boy system at work.

Did she still have political clout because her husband was an ex-president and she had challenged Obama in the primaries? Of course. How do you turn an enemy into a supporter? Remember how the animosity between Republicans Abraham Lincoln and William Seward was eliminated? Right, the good ole boy system.

If you get a political appointment because you're a relative, John Kennedy appointing brother Bobby Attorney General, it's called nepotism.

How does it involve the electorate? It doesn't. Step way back.

Did you vote for the vice president, Joe Biden, the second most powerful person in the world, or was he picked by a party and candidate? Did you vote for the third person in line for the presidency, the Speaker of the House, currently Republican Paul Ryan? No, not unless you're from his state, and even then that vote was for a seat in the House of Representatives, not a seat at the door of the White House.

Have you ever voted to install a cabinet member? Say, secretaries of Agriculture, Commerce, Defense, Education, Energy, Health and Human Services, Homeland Security, Housing and Urban Development, Interior, Labor, State, Transportation, Treasury, and Veterans Affairs?

Get it? We voters are out the door, down the steps and on the curb as bystanders when it comes to national presidential elections and DC leadership selections. And we wonder why things are out of control and national priorities are replaced by political ambitions.

What now? In an unprecedented move, the Democratic and Republican parties' top guns met and agreed to promote legislation to lower the barriers that hinder voters' voices from being heard during elections.

The Democrats especially want to eliminate the Electoral College, since it has cost them seats behind the desk in the Oval Office for both Hillary Clinton and Al Gore.

--Sam Grogan, Columnist for Ersatz News

Latest Poll: Rich on the Outs

Chicago: Ersatz News and Views—'we live up to our name'
The latest Nelson Polls show that being middle class is IN and being rich is OUT.

Since President Reagan took office, being rich has been the envy of most people. The glamourous, glitzy, no-rules, lavish, Hollywood lifestyle has been the rage. Trickle-down economics turned out truly to be a trickle or maybe a drip.

But now, with the two top candidates for the last presidential election both gaining wealth by questionable means, amassing a fortune is not so popular with the everyday public.

According to Chicago accountant Carrie Nickels, "When looked at closely, both candidates seemed sleazy compared to the endeavor of the average middleclass worker. Where's their ethics? Where's their transparency."

Now, instead of seeing the rich as cool, you hear *miser, materialist, glutton, scrooge* and other nouns associated with those who make and hide more money than they can ever spend while often disregarding those they hurt on the way to riches. And their methods are questioned especially if they hire workers to do their everyday dirty work while paying minimum wage.

Making millions while limiting their employees to part-time hours so that they don't have to help pay for insurance is also an issue, show the polls. That caused Congress to pass a socialize medicine bill which is now under reform.

"If you sat at a table and one person had a ham, turkey, whole prime rib and fixings in front of him, while the other diners at the table were eating spaghetti, you'd call him gross," said Betty Sheldmyer, Cleveland housewife. "That's the way I feel when I read about people with 5,000 sq. ft. mansions, jet planes, half million dollar cars and a yacht. It's gross. It's not beautiful, it's ugly."

"Most members of Congress are rich and living a luxurious life in Washington. They don't have a worry," mentions Nate Wells, self-employed contractor. "I make a good living, pay my taxes, and expect congress to at least come up with a health bill for everyone that doesn't cost an arm and a leg. Obamacare was unworkable and proposals to fix it by congress are worse. Hey, we don't want to worry either."

The polls also show a distain for glorifying movie and rock stars. According to businessman Sammy Cotton, "If any of the media stories are true, stars, both movie and rock, are embarrassing. Alcoholism, drug addiction, early death, overdosing, disregard for marital vows, filthy lyrics and movies, and wasteful spending are no longer behaviors to admire. At least I hope they aren't. This is the 21st Century, for goodness sake. We're tired of Lalaland."

How to Increase the Chances Your Child Will Reach Adulthood

By Dr. Jonah Hamilton, Ersatz News Special Contributor

Kids want thrills, but real thrills outside of the Disney universe often are dangerous. So, don't buy them skateboards and allow them to slide down steel railings and fly off ramps. If you buy a trampoline, make sure it's strong, safe and supervised.

Most teen deaths are caused by accidents, as you probably imagined. Of those, automobile accidents are the cause of about two-thirds or more.

Hold off getting your child a driver's license as long as you can, especially if you have a boy. Many more young males die in car accidents than girls. Boys are obsessed by prowess and often choose a car or motorcycle to try to prove their manhood versus using their brains and brawn.

Remember, most boys in the rest of the world don't drive. The ones that do in Western countries can't obtain a license until they are 18, and then it costs thousands of dollars.

If it's imperative that a teen have a car, make it a slow, large, safe car. Don't buy a muscle car, sports car or anything with a V6 or V8. That's just asking for your son to speed, race, show off and drive recklessly.

Consider the animals who are killed by the 10s of thousands on the roads each day. They can't image a thing so awkward, fast and out of control that that it cannot avoid animals peacefully traveling from one feeding ground to another.

If your child attends public school, make them ride the bus. It's much safer than you driving them or having them drive themselves. The less any family member is on the road, the safer you all are.

If your community has busses, subways, trams and other transportation, teach your teen how to use them. A boy and a girl taking the bus to a movie and fast food dinner is much safer than driving around for hours. Approximately 35,000 Americans die in automobile accidents each year.

Home schooling is one way to avoid the negative influences of peers, many of which are harmful. In many countries the children eat meals with their parents, work beside them learning a trade, sleep in the same room with them and so forth. That means until the children marry and leave the home their main influences are the adults they live and work with. Also, dating is often a group affair to a teen night club.

Therefore there is little peer pressure from a subculture that promotes defying parents, using alcohol, experimenting with drugs, committing crimes and participating in early sexual acts. We wonder why many kids living in American don't want to grow up and act like adults.

Parents often hand a boy the keys to a car and then another set of parents lets their 16-year-old daughter get into a car with him and disappear for five or more hours. What do you expect they will do unsupervised? The results are predictable. Have your children conduct their dating in your home or the home of other parents who are in the house.

Don't send your child to a residential university unless you live in that town. If you think letting a dating couple have five hours alone every weekend is unwise, think about what happens when you put 25 to 40 thousand adolescents and young adults in the same neighborhood for 8 months unsupervised. That's right, literally big, reckless, drunken orgies at fraternities and off-campus apartments. Many parents, for comfort, will tell themselves, "Not my child." If everyone is saying that, then whose child?

Congress Plans to Stop Favoring Support of Big Cities over Rural Areas

ERSATZ NEWS WASHINGTON—'living up to our name'

Several House and Senate bills are in committee now that address the disproportionate support urban areas receive from the Federal government versus rural areas.

"Of course cities need lots of cash," says Senator Fred Nathan of Utah. "But we have to remember that cities are our seats of Capitalism. Big banks, billion dollar real estate firms, national insurance agencies, and Fortune 500 companies should be able to support their cities. Why would these capitalist-controlled cities have to ask the government for help?"

Cal Stephenson, U.S. Representative from Indiana, comments, "The cities tend to be more liberal and socialistic concerning ideology, asking for more money every year for social programs. In my state, most of the towns and cities contain conservatives who believe in working to support themselves and are embarrassed to take charity. They don't want to be on welfare."

"Even with that, many towns through service organizations, churches and local charities attempt to support those in need without state or local governmental help," adds Stephenson. "That doesn't mean, though, the federal government should send most of the entitlement money to urban areas. That encourages laziness, or what some call 'enabling' bad behavior. Examples are wasting money that should be spent for their family's necessities on alcohol, drugs, lottery tickets, etc."

"Look, I'm a liberal and realize that American is very close to being a socialist country. A lot of people would be unhappy without Social Security, Medicare, Medicaid, Food Stamps, Earned Income Tax Credit, Supplemental Security Income, Affordable Care Act, Housing Assistance, unemployment benefits, public schools, school lunch programs, state colleges, and other socialist programs," states Senator Greg Colson. "But we need to slow down. You can't become a socialist country overnight if you're the size of the United State. It's too shocking for people to take. When programs develop a little at a time, the blowback is spread out and socialism becomes acceptable."

One large city mayor that refused to let us use his name replied to these comments: "Hogwash. Cities are where most of the crime, poverty, infrastructure needs and jobless citizens are. They need federal support to meet the demand from a large population of the down and out. I'm pushing our state's representatives in Washington to increase our benefits."

For a Change, Good News about Fast Food Restaurants

ERSATZ SCIENCE NEWS—'living up to our name'

Living near a fast food restaurant can be healthful, according to a recently publish doctoral dissertation.

Anna Colberg, PHD from UNC, issued the results of her research in *Good Health, Good Life* magazine this fall.

Her four-year study of families living close enough to restaurants to easily smell the evaporating fat from deep fryer exhausts, revealed some health benefits.

Colberg said in a phone interview: "The most notable aspect of the oil in the air is the sheen in the hair of family members. No artificial hair creams or oils were needed to keep their hair looking healthy. Plus, no one in the test group complained of dandruff."

She also mentioned that fewer members of the tested families suffered from eczema or dry skin than control groups outside the range of particulates from fast food and other restaurants. The cosmetic use of petroleum, animal and vegetable fats, plant extracts and chemically produced fragrances was lower in the 'fast food' group.

"People in my test group had fewer reports of constipation. In fact the benefits were as good as studies of patients that took regular doses of mineral oil," added Colberg.

The article, "Fast Food for Thought," includes charts proving that people living next to fast food restaurants tended to eat lower amounts of deep fried foods than the control group because the smell from the restaurants had become noxious enough to dampen their appetites.

'Pay your own way' is motto of new republican congress members

ERSATZ NEWS—'living up to our name'

"It's troubling when our constituents complain to us that money needs to be spent on roads, public transportation, education, etc. and at the same time warn us not to raise taxes," states Tom Hamilton, Republican member of the House of Representatives.

Charlene Dauws, Republican senator, added, "A few pennies tacked onto each gallon of gas would do wonders. So would a federal sales tax.

"For some reason people who pay for products and services every day in their neighborhoods want free services from the fed. They don't go into stores or the auto repair shop and leave without paying. That would be unheard of.

"We can't just keep running up the national debt, which is over 20,000,000,000,000 now, and pretend money grows on trees."

This thinking has come into the congress from newly elected Republican representatives. The question is: "Will the old Republican guard change the system they have been under for years?"

Abraham Amstic, Ersatz News political analyst, answers: "These new congressmen and women don't have a chance. The ranking Republican congressmen and women have been spoiled by spending whatever they want and not creating and following a realistic federal budget.

"That's how they remain popular with their districts and get re-elected. The more they run up the national debt to supply 'free' social services, the happier their local citizens are with them."

No doubt the battle between the "no tax entitlement" people and the "fiscally responsible" crowd will continue, but Republican congressional freshmen and women plan to make some, what they call "sensible," waves as they try to get Americans to pay their own way.

Weinland College undergrads stage protest over end of athletic scholarships

Ersatz News—'living up to its name'

A demonstration on the steps of the Administration Building at Weinland College blocked Chancellor Howard Eplee from going to work yesterday morning.

The cause of the protest was the end to the school's 53 years of providing their NCAA Division 1 athletes scholarships.

Only less than 200 of the school's 9,481 students braved the cold and snowy morning, but their message was made clear on signs and during chants: "Down with Eplee at WC," "Students at Weinland support their Eland," "No no, athletics won't go."

The giant eland is the school's mascot.

Eplee, who returned calls to Ersatz News, says, "I understand the students' concerns; athletic events are fun, promote school spirit and provide some educational opportunities for special students, but most of those benefits can be had without paid athletes. So now, instead of participating in Division I, we will compete with Division III schools, which also don't award athletic scholarships."

"Of course, I don't make rule changes like this. That's why universities have a board of directors. They voted unanimously on this issue. They wanted to put the focus of Weinland back on academics while still letting students enjoy college athletics," continued the chancellor.

One student, Nate Hadley, who was a bystander to the demonstration, commented: "The emphasis on athletics in America is way out of proportion, so I like what Weinland is doing. Why lower academic standards for skilled athletics and then provide them with full-ride scholarships! Our best basketball and football players never graduate. They just use Weinland as a stepping stone to the pros or have to be tutored heavily so they won't flunk out."

Coed Shaman Drake partially disagreed: "I don't want the Elands to play unknown basketball teams, but I do dislike the practice of letting athletes cheat their way through college with the staff's help. I sit next to a football player in World Civ II and someone else is in his seat and takes his tests during exams. That's just wrong."

Hadley added, "And tutors do research for them and write their term papers. I have a class with one of the tutors who told me that's how she pays for her dorm room. Didn't UNC get exposed by CNN for recruiting athletes who couldn't read or write?"

Eplee listed some of the schools Weinland might play, "Amherst, Tufts, John Hopkins, Carnegie and MIT, if they field teams that correspond with ours. I know the excitement at a basketball game is greater when occasionally Weinland gets to play a Duke or Indiana in the March tourney, but, we need priorities.

"The board and I want Weinland to be recognized as a great institution of higher learning. Many universities are only known as a football or basketball school. That's not what we want."

Protestor Greg Matthews said, "Eplee has forgotten what it's like to be young, a college student. He needs to rip loose once in a while and then he wouldn't make stupid decisions like this one."

One professor related that "it's sad that amateur sports have become professional. Somehow we let the fact that Russia and other teams cheated and paid their Olympic athletes convince us to pay all our athletics.

"Most secondary schools in other countries don't have school sponsored sports. Athletics, besides gym class, are club sports after school and supported by parents or participants."

"The students will get over this when they realize that sporting events will be as entertaining as usual. Since the only person's name people recognize from some major universities is the basketball or football coach, I hope our students will be proud we made the decision to be known for our academics and not an athletic teams," concluded Eplee.

Onboard Driving Monitor Tested

Ersatz News—'it lives up to its name'

Jim Hancock of Bedford received a shock last week when his engine trouble light came on and started blinking. Then the onboard computer told him that he must pull over in a safe place within two minutes to protect the car's engine.

"I freaked out. I pulled over as quickly as I could and shut off the engine," said Hancock. "I didn't know what to think, because my car is new. How could anything go wrong so soon?"

Next Hancock's car's digital assistant said, "Don't worry, help will arrive shortly." Waiting for a wrecker or a "road ranger" mechanic, Hancock was surprised when a state policeman arrived. He told the officer his problem, but the officer ignored his explanation and asked for his driver's license and car registration.

After the trouper checked those documents in his car, Hancock explained that the officer told him he was going to receive a ticket for speeding and reckless driving. "I was confused. I had been speeding, but what did that have to do with my engine light coming on?"

Hancock went on to explain and a little research backed up his story. He was told by the officer that he had been caught by a new built-in device labeled (IDentify-Illegal-Overall Traffic).

The Transport Federal Board convinced every automaker operating in America to put this monitor in one out of every 1,000 cars as a pilot program. Hancock was unlucky enough to buy one of the test vehicles.

TFB director Lacia Gonzalez explained how it works: "The monitor, using a GPS, tracks the speed and location of a driver's automobile, just like your built-in or portable GPS can show you the current speed limit of the road you're on, tell that you've turned and indicate that you're traveling so many miles an hour.

"It logs this information to see whether what appears to be speeding and switching lanes recklessly is a habit or an occasional maneuver to avoid a road hazard or pass a car. If it's not habitual, nothing happens. If it is a habit, the automobile's assistant may tell the driver to pull over.

"If the occurrences are regular and about the same time each weekday, let's say morning rush hour, the monitor's algorithm concludes that the driver probably is always late getting up to drive to work."

She went on to explain that when the data is sufficiently incriminating the monitor notifies 911 and the nearest police officer is dispatched to the car's location. He then issues a ticket. If the driver doesn't heed the trouble indicator light and voice command, the auto's computer starves the engine of gas. The reduced RPMs slow the car and the driver has to pull over.

"I guess it's like the old governors that were on farm engines and some trucks. Those kept the motors from over revving and blowing up," added Hancock. "I don't know if this device is legal or not. I'm sure someone will test it in court. I'm not going to. I just paid my fine and try to be a better driver."

Gonzalez is hoping that eventually all cars will be equipped with the monitor, but she knows that it won't be popular with those who like to drive illegally, ignoring speed limits and safe breaking distances between cars."

When asked if the name of the device (ID-I-OT monitor) was a double entendre, Gonzalez didn't reply.

GOP Seeking New Name

By Quen Dawkins, *Ersatz News*—'it lives up to its name'

Ever since the Democratic Party started using the label progressive instead of liberal, the Republicans have been looking for a new name too.

"I can see why Democrats wanted to stop being called liberals," says Ersatz News political analyst Sue Towers. "It smacks of being a spendthrift, sexually promiscuous, lacking cultural standards—basically believing people can make up the rules as they go along."

Jon Jones, a county democratic leader, stated: "We received the liberal label rightly some time ago because we were the first to embrace a woman's right to choose to abort a fetus, same-sex marriages and most of the existing social programs. The conservatives fought against these. We took the country forward and had to drag the conservatives along."

Republican state chairperson Donald Fosbrink says, "The Democrats adopted progressive as a euphemism when liberal fit them more accurately. By labeling themselves progressive the implication was that the conservatives were reactionary. We need to counter that, because I don't like our philosophical opponents dictating our image."

The Republican Party has a list of possible titles: the sensible, pragmatic, utilitarian, ethical, realistic or commonsense party.

Fosbrink went on to explain that "if the Republicans use a euphemism, such as sensible, the implication is that the other party lacks common sense in its actions. What goes around comes around—right?"

Towers commented that "this is just more political posturing. The problem is that it often works because the voters don't stop to analyze the two parties' actions. The whole thing is divisive without carrying much meaning.

"For example, you'd think the conservatives would be better staying within a budget, but the data shows that one party is just as liberal with money as the other."

Both parties try to push the Constitution to its limits and beyond, mentioned Towers. It's no wander most citizens outside the Beltway are disappointed in government. We need less verbiage and more actions from our representatives in Washington. Who cares what the two parties call themselves if nothing gets done because the parties are jockeying for power and growing fat from corruption."

According to Towers, two questions remain: which word will the Republicans use to describe their perceived philosophy? Fosbrink favors calling conservatives realists. And, will the progressives counter with a different flattering label for themselves?

Global Warming? Real Manmade? Maybe

ERSATZ NEWS AND VIEWS—'living up to its name'

There are plenty of scientific studies proving that global warming is happening. The debate comes when groups try to identify causes and assign blame.

Some say that burning fossil fuels (coal) is the major reason for increased greenhouse gasses in the atmosphere. Others blame gas-burning vehicles, whose use has spread from rich nations in the West to the economically advancing China and the subcontinent of India, two of the largest populated areas in the world.

The methane released from animals, especially large herds of cattle we raise for beef, has also come under question.

If global warming is manmade, how does the average citizen understand and deal with their share of the problem.

Ed Howser, chairman of International Studies at Higgins Technological Institute, says one important task is researching the sources of information: "If a homeowner is receiving alarming mail about global warming while asking for donations, he should be cautious about believing the message. If an organization's income is tied to a problem, guess what, they will play the fear card, predicting the next biblical flood, or the sympathy card about the demise of a small animal."

Of course, when you follow the money, you may also find those earning their livelihood in the meat or coal industry telling their opinions, right or wrong, about the issue.

He went on to suggest people who want to donate should check out how much of the contributed money goes to the director, headquarters' buildings, fundraising and staff and then how much goes for the cause. Charities have become a safer way to get rich quick and are far less dangerous than Ponzi schemes. Some nonprofit organizations' CEOs make hundreds of thousands of dollars.

Galvestone Gazzette environmental journalist wrote: "Most older citizens remember when some of the current charities began. They were 99% volunteer organizations. Over 50 plus years they turned into big businesses that require millions just to exist, which means the cause receives a smaller percentage of funds each year. The bigger the organization the more suspicious donors should become, because it becomes easier to slip some cash donations and checks out the "back door." Creative bookkeeping and embezzlement also become more likely, and most companies won't prosecute offenders because bad publicity about the handling of donations causes donors to mistrust a nonprofit. Then they stop donating."

Don't believe what any expert, professor or fundraiser says if they are making a living by promoting a cause. Long time nongovernmental organization worker and charity employee Sam Falon says, "I worked in a foreign country at an NGO that focused on providing nourishing meals for starving children.

"The local manager of the organization had no other job, yet he had a house, car and fine clothing far above that of his neighbors, most of which had no cars.

"I Googled to see how the US parent organization was rated by a charity watchdog group. It had received an A. The pie chart showed that only 8% of the donated money went for fundraising, offices, staff and other overhead.

"That was a surprise because I knew that the US headquarters deducted 15% from the total grant before the funds were sent to us. We used 60% of the money they sent for our overhead and staff. I don't know what the manager took for his personal use, but that meant less than 34 % of the original funds were used to feed children. We workers were not allowed to see any books."

Falon explained that often the watchdogs use information supplied to them by the charities, information that only supports their opinions. And, even if the watchdogs used public or government records, the nonprofits can "fix the books," just as many individual citizens and for-profit companies fail to report income to the IRS. Think of Madoff and Enron. It took years for them go get caught.

Alaskan scholar Howard Downes says the chief way organizations try to alarm donors is by directing attention to retreating glaciers: "Anyone who has read John Muir, founder of the Sierra Club, knows that he reported that some glaciers in Alaska had shrunk by 20 or 30 miles already by the time he visited them in the late 1800s. You don't read that in environmental organization's requests for donations."

Downes went on to point out that that would have been when the earth's population was much smaller and cars, airplanes and electric generation were in the experimental stages. That leaves bovines and other
animals, plus the eruption of volcanoes, as the culprits for the dwindling Alaskan glaciers.

Then there's the question of how serious is the population of America taking global warning. A study by Environ Research Coalition titled <u>How Worried Are We about Global Warming? Not very!</u> "People are still buying six- and eight-cylinder trucks and SUVs even if they only drive them to the office, not to a construction site, mining operation or farm yard. If they own a four-cylinder vehicle, it is often supercharged.

"They're still driving a 2,000 lb. vehicle to the grocery for a gallon of milk, a pound loaf of bread and a package of hamburger instead of taking public transportation, walking or bicycling to the nearest convenience store.

"They're still overheating and cooling their houses instead of adjusting the layers of clothing they are wearing.

"They're still bulldozing thousands of forests and grasslands and covering them with streets, houses, patios and driveways so that they can have their single dwelling instead of living in a high-rise.

"They're still eating meat at almost every meal, something that most people in the world are unable to do or afford.

"Does that sound like they are very concerned about the ozone layer, rising sea levels and the extinction of endangers animals?

<u>Scientific Consumer</u> staff member Joy Workman wrote in an editorial: "One political party likes to use climate change as a rallying cry. Well, tell me who's to blame for the Ice Age, a catastrophic global cooling."

Was that caused by a national leader? Maybe it was the result, ironically, from a *lack* of cattle, no cars and the absence of burning coal?"

Plus wasn't there a global warming after the Ice Age? Who caused that?"

It takes significant study to understand global issues. I wish we could trust those writing dissertations and books, but we've learned not to trust those seeking doctorates or having to publish or perish. They've scientifically proven that eggs are bad for you one year and then determined that they're good for you ten years later. After another ten years a third scientist will prove eggs bad for you again.

"The problem is that they have to find something new to prove, and since they can't, they just disagree with a previous finding. It may make it easy for them to do some epidemiological studies to 'support' their thesis, but that doesn't help us at all when we try to understand environmental issues. Who is correct then? What can we believe? How can we change our behavior to help the environment if we can't trust the 'experts'?"

Elementary School Dismantles Playground

Behind Thomas Jefferson Elementary School in Hobokan, you'll not find a ballfield, soccer field, playground or basketball courts. All you'll see are several mounds of dirt or sand, random logs and a pile of cut boards. The playground equipment that was once there is gone

Traditional school playgrounds feature metal and plastic slides, swings, steel monkey bars, plastic platforms and other manmade items. Jefferson has chosen to go back in time and just have dirt, branched trees, ponds and planks.

"Our kids come from normal middle class families, which means they spend much of their discretionary time on a sofa, bed or floor with a digital screen or two in front of them," says Principal Sandy Canfield. "They seldom leave the house, and if they do, many parents don't want them to get dirty or damage a carefully manicured lawn. So there are no dirt piles or mud holes in the back yard to experiment with."

"Kids are little scientists, so playing is their personal way of educating themselves to the world around them," adds fifth-grade teacher Tomi Robbins. "It's great that they can vicariously explore the digital world in this day and age, but being able to deal with real objects and terrain is also good. I like the environment we have behind the school. We tore down our traditional play equipment years ago."

The children at Jefferson must put on goggles and then they can play in the five-foot high and 12-foot square sand pile, run around or over the 10-foot high dirt mound, experiment in a flowing ditch or splash around in one of the pools of water. One pond contained fish, another had kids floating paper or wooden boats and a third was just for wading. The ditch was being dammed with mud and rocks and experimented with using wood chips or other buoyant items.

Counselor Harry Corkran says, "I like that there are no preconceived uses for the items in our playground. A swing is a swing and a slide is a slide. With our play area the kids make up their own games and activities. Of course they play tag, race each other climbing a tree or mound, roll or slide down the hills, swing or climb on a rope and work together to build forts with the planks."

Principal Canfield mentioned that they don't have any balls, bats, racquets, nets or other organized game equipment on the premises. The reason, she explained, is because those are plentiful at their homes and are usually molding and deflating in a box in the garage. Plus, those manmade items have been taken from the sandlot to fields built by coaches and parents that supervise their use.

"The kids wading must quit early and rinse off, and those playing in the dry dirt or sand must leave their goggles on and walk through a double fan, kind of like those at a car wash, before re-entering the school," added Canfield. "We don't mind the kids getting dirty or tracking in a little sand, our custodial staff sweeps every evening."

"We have no need for a gym teacher or Phys. Ed. classes," says Corkran. "It's amazing what an overall workout our students get in our more natural play area. A few parents won't let their children use our area because they don't want them climbing trees or getting mud or grass stains on their expensive clothing, so we have these children read books in the library or do calisthenics in the classroom while the others play outside. "

Of course we have teachers and paraprofessionals in the area during recesses, but they don't direct activities. They're just there so kids play safely."

Canfield says, "We haven't had any requests to return to traditional playground equipment. Maybe that's because there are about five parks in town with those, and they're usually used by preschool children or not used at all.

--Sandy Jones, Ersatz News—'living up to its name'

NCAA Floats Ethnicity Rule for Athletic Teams

ERSATZ Sports--Indianapolis

To make sure basketball teams represent the ethnicity and academic standards of NCAA university students, new rules are being considered. If the first rule passes, a team's makeup will have to be within one player of the average ethnicity percentage of the general student body.

One large-conference team, which was the most representative of all 12 teams, has 73% Blacks on the team whereas the student body has less than 5%. Both Hispanic and Asian students at the university had above the Black percentage but were not represented on the team.

Plus no Native Americans or Hawaiian/Pacific Islanders were represented, which is not surprising since their representation in the general student body was approximately 0.1% each. Even by adding multi-racial to the black percentage the total would still be under 10% or one Black for every ten players.

The new rule, if adopted, would mean that our sample basketball team, which last year had 15 players on its roster, would consist of 1 Black, 1 Asian, 1 Hispanic and 12 white players.

When asked if the high percentage of Black players in relation to white ones was due to affirmative action, the president replied: "That's a whole different issue and doesn't apply to our discussion. We're interested in the talent and experience exhibited by our students. So we recruit the best players we can find no matter their ethnicity."

Another rule that is being discussed contains a clause that states that the incoming recruited basketball players' average SAT score must be within 50 or above points in relation to the average student body SAT score.

Concerning the second rule, the president commented, "Looking for the best students also holds true for our academic admission standards." Records show that the average SAT score of entering freshmen was 120 to 250 points higher than the average of recruited basketball players. The president related that he hadn't seen those statistics.

Retired Division I assistant basketball Coach Bart Holcomb said, "The colleges where I worked always fudged on athletes' admission standards. If the administration couldn't manipulate the SAT or ACT numbers, they made up waivers, held summer college-prep make-up classes and/or hired tutors."

"You can tell how much numbers mean to NCAA basketball when the Big Ten has fourteen teams," said Holcomb, laughing.

"You can be sure these athletes who came out of high school poorly prepared for college have their papers written by paid student ghost writers or paid tutors," continued Holcomb. "Some of my players only attended classes the first and last days of the semester. We had paid test takers occupy some of our athletes' seats during quizzes, midterms and finals. Any member of the student body who had a class with one of these athletes was well aware of what was going on. Professors, on the other hand, looked the other way."

DOD to Become DOO?

ERSATZNEWS—WASHINGTON—'living up to its name'

No one in Washington can remember defense being America's prime concern, claims liberal organization STOP. So its members want to change the name of the Department of Defense to the Department of Offense. They go on to assert that federal records show America spends more than the next 10 developed nations combined on its military--the most expensive items being offensive weapons.

Most don't agree with a name change, though, as proclaimed by Congresswoman Sandra McCullough, participant in a recent forum in D.C.: "Changing the name would send the wrong message, but I do wish we spent more on defending from attack and not so much on weapons of mass destruction. I think this campaign is just a gimmick to get attention and raise money for STOP."

"Americans are always surprised that many people in the world hate America," commented international affairs expert Cowen Salienti and STOP chairman. "That's because we think everything we do internationally is to help others. We're the good guys.

"Yes, they call for help when things go astray in their country, but the rest of the time they want to be left alone." Salienti went on to express how upset our citizens were when they thought Russia might have interfered in our 2016 election. Then he shuffled though his briefcase, pulled out a sheet of paper and passed it around the table. It listed America's attempts at regime change before, during or after these countries' elections:

China 1949 to early 1960s, Albania 1949-53, East
Germany 1950s, Iran 1953, Guatemala 1954, Costa
Rica mid-1950s, Syria 1956-7, Egypt 1957, Indonesia
1957-8, British Guiana 1953-64, Iraq 1963, North
Vietnam 1945-73, Cambodia 1955-70, Laos 1958,
Ecuador 1960-63, Congo 1960, France 1965, Brazil
1962-64, Dominican Republic 1963, Cuba 1959 to
present, Bolivia 1964, Indonesia 1965, Ghana 1966,
Chile 1964-73, Greece 1967, Costa Rica 1970-71,
Bolivia 1971, Australia 1973-75, Angola 1975, Zaire
1975, Portugal 1974-76, Jamaica 1976-80, Seychelles
1979-81, Chad 1981-82, Grenada 1983, South Yemen
1982-84, Suriname 1982-84, Fiji 1987, Libya 1980s,
Nicaragua 1981-90, Panama 1989, Bulgaria 1990,
Albania 1991, Iraq 1991, Afghanistan 1980s, Somalia
1993, Yugoslavia 1999-2000, Ecuador 2000,
Afghanistan 2001, Venezuela 2002, Iraq 2003, Haiti
2004, Somalia 2007 to present, Libya 2011, Syria
2012 to present.

"This list speaks for itself," he said.

Block State University Professor James T. Higgins commented on list: "And the sad part is that most of the regime changes led to worse conditions in those countries and sometimes the whole region. Take Iraq for example. We wanted to get rid of Saddam Hussein, but we destroyed the water, electrical, gas and road infrastructure of the capital city, all while killing thousands of Iraqi soldiers who were caught between a dictator's threats and America's military. They had few ways to escape death. Our actions greatly harmed civilians, kids, moms, grandparents and local businessmen."

On the other hand, Fredrick Nemor, former ambassador to several Middle East nations, says, "Look how stable Iraq, Iran, Libya, Pakistan and Afghanistan are now. What if America had never taken on the challenge of making these countries democracies?"

"I don't know where you've been, Nemor, but these countries are anything but democracies. The damage done in Iraq spread to neighboring Syria. The Arab Spring so many politicians bragged about has been a disaster," commented Higgins. "Democracy has to come from the ground up, not from another nation's military, economic and political pressure. These Arab and other tribes have never worked closely together because their goals, cultures, religions and political systems are light years apart. They don't like capitalism and democracy. They like small tribal governance, not some politician in the capital city dictating about concerns that make no sense at the local level."

Higgins continued: "I don't know what Americans think the CIA does. But their job is to gather information. Do people believe that only China and Russia hack other countries' servers? Google America hacking Iran, Russia, China and North Korea."

Nemor claims that America doesn't hack other countries, and says "the claims that we hacked to shut down some of Iran's nuclear centrifuges are Iranian propaganda to make the United Nation countries think poorly of America's international actions and cover up Iran's own inability to enrich uranium properly.

Forum member Janice Westerman added, "I've tried to analyze America's political actions around the world to determine whether it's offensive or defensive—kind of to see the USA from a foreign country's point of view and compare it to what I would think if another country were treating us as America treats them.

"Ok, would I like foreign drones flying over Texas and firing missiles? Would it be ok with Americans if we had Japanese, German and Cuban bases in the United States? Would it be ok with us if a country that was mad at us bypassed the United Nations and starting bombing an America city? When Russia invades Georgia or the Ukraine, we get upset. What did we expect Russia to do when we invaded Syria, Iraq, Afghanistan, Libya, Somalia, and so forth? I wouldn't like it at all, so how can I expect them to."

Lacy Jackson, moderator, summed up the event by saying that the forum ended with both sides holding to their positions and the name change issue mostly ignored.

Seattle Residents Sell Their Vehicles, Buy Bicycles

ERSATZ News and Views—'we live up to our name'

Those wanting a great buy on a used automobile should immediately go to Seattle. A rally to encourage citizens to add action to lip service about global warming has resulted in thousands of area residents selling their cars and trucks and buying bicycles and/or using public transportation.

Sally James, one of the Clear Air Rally (CAR) organizers, says, "I'm so proud of our citizens. Many people just complain about global warming and then continue to drive big trucks, SUVs, V8 cars and motorcycles as if they're not part of the problem."

So far, James claims, over 10,000 people have signed a pledge to either sell their vehicle or, at least, not use it during the week. Riding a bicycle or walking to work was another option on the pledge.

Although the CAR gathering focused on reducing the pollution caused by refining oil, vehicle emissions, automobile factories, electric generation for hybrid cars and steel production, turning down the heat in winter and A/C in summer were also encouraged.

The rally took place a week ago, and one of the side benefits is that already the usual traffic problems have decreased. This is especially significant since some reports list Seattle as the 2nd worst city in the US for evening rush-hour traffic.

President Backpedals on Border Wall Position

ERSATZ NEWS, ALMIAS RIOS CIUDAD

In a move that surprised many, President Trump halted his order to begin working on the wall between the United States and Mexico.

Protests, lawsuits and worldwide criticism have made the President rethink the extreme measure he had first suggested. Some opponents of the wall suggest that the Trump presidency take down the 600 miles of fencing and wall erected on the border during the tenure of former presidents.

Suggestions have even been made not only to take down the existing barriers but to also remove thousands of motion sensors and cut back on border control officers. Their reasoning is that you can't keep illegal aliens out of the United States, so why waste the money.

Those worried about an increased illegal drug supply without border control don't have a point, says DEA officer Cam Staller, "If Americans want the drugs, Mexico, Colombia and other countries will make sure they have them. We can't blame foreigners. The production, transport and sale of drugs is caused by our neighbors and children. Trying to stop suppliers is like taking aspirin as a cancer cure. The underlying cause is the greater problem."

Currently photos of the border show everything from fencing a person can step over to 15 foot high concrete, steel beam or razor wire walls that can't completely stop an intruder but make crossing illegally into the United State very difficult.

Of course Texas, Arizona, New Mexico and California residents living near the border are those most affected by incursions and therefor want the 600 miles of wall and fencing lengthened and reinforced to make it more difficult to breach. Many border communities have set up vigilante groups to monitor the border where the US border patrols are two widespread to be effective.

After Candidate Trump mentioned beefing up border security during the campaign, Mexican border towns became and still are overwhelmed with those wanting to enter America. Besides Mexicans, citizens of Central American countries lead the list, especially Nicaraguan and Guatemalan.

Plus, those who have been deported to Mexico often live in make-shift border settlements awaiting a second or third chance to sneak over the border, which only adds to the border towns' problems.

"Those who want to break the immigration laws or immigrate to America without extensive vetting," says Arizonan Todd Braxton, "are not very happy with Trump. I'm not sure why Americans aren't saying, 'It's about time a president took appropriate action as the person in charge of executing our laws, which includes securing our borders.'"

"Trump is an embarrassment. Years of progress are being erased by his dictatorial mandates and executive actions," countered New Yorker Dane Howard. "Does he want America to look like the Soviet Union during the Cold War? Trump, take down that wall!"

The Mexican government has no interest in a wall. NAFTA produced tens of thousands of good paying jobs close to the Mexican side of the border. That money is paid in Mexico and stays in Mexico.

Having citizens who were unemployed leave Mexico and travel legally or illegally to the US is a win-win situation for Mexico. Immigrants send millions of US dollars back to families who spend it in Mexico and Mexico's percentage of unemployment decreases.

Of course the Mexican government is angry with the new American politics. If Trump makes the promised changes, Mexico will suffer.

"We should share the wealth," states farmer John Fraser of Ohio. "We take unfair advantage of natural resources from around the world and love buying cheap goods produced by underpaid foreign labor. We're such hypocrites in America. We even pretend to buy 'America First' products while driving our Toyota and fixing the faucet with a Chinese wrench."

U.S. Tech Deficiency

ERSATZ News and Views—'living up to its name'

With all the news coverage about Russia hacking emails and releasing damaging details of Hillary Clinton's campaign, questions have arisen concerning the NSA, FBI and CIA's abilities to function effectively in the tech world of the 21st Century.

"We have been focused on bombing and occupying dozens of countries that we are in disagreement with, but our tactics haven't improved situations," says an anonymous source. "Drone attacks and assassinations of top foreign officials sound good, but what affect have they had. Political chaos and long wars."

The source went on to explain that the CIA and FBI are way behind in cyber warfare. Indicating that we still don't know whether exposing the backroom tactics of the Clinton camp changed the outcome of the election, while Putin may be laughing at our ineptitude.

With the recent airing on the History Channel of a documentary showing how President Ronald Reagan, Vice President George Bush, NSC's Oliver North, Caspar Weinberger, John Poindexter and Robert McFarlane engineered the illegal selling of arms to Iran, an enemy, to fund the Contras in Nicaragua, demonstrating just how underhanded and incompetent US leaders and departments can be.

Many of the participants when indicted or convicted in the Iran-Contra affair were pardoned by President George H. W. Bush.

So, according to the anonymous source, "the intelligence agencies are red in the face again." Many Americans assume that besides assassinations, wars and occupations America is also hacking into foreign elections to make them correspond to its wishes just as America suspects Russia of doing. That seems to not be the case since there is so much ado over the alleged Russian "hacking" during the recent presidential election.

Is Our National Anthem Offensive?

ERSATZ NEWS AND VIEWS—'we live up to our name'
Indianola, SC

"And the rocket's red glare, the bombs bursting in air," is being considered by several small liberal organizations as too offensive to the modern image of the United States of America.

Political correctness has become a big issue in the last several decades, which has meant not using certain terms to identify other races, nationalities, sports teams and women.

Negro has been replaced by African American and Black. Indian has become First Nation or Native Americans.

Actress has been replaced with actor for both genders, and stewardess and waitress have become steward and server.

Sports teams have been criticized for their names because liberal groups have found that names such as Redskins--which, along with Black, are examples of Synecdoche or Metonymy--and Red Devils and Blue Devils are religiously offensive.

In the past statues and memorials to brave leaders of the South's efforts at self-determination were pulled down all over the nation because they were deemed racist.

So, it's no surprise that the National Anthem is under fire for being unPC, bellicose.

"We should be singing about our peace loving patriots, being a republic and a capitalist nation, not bombing and killing," stated Sandra Cole, president of Make It Right (MIR). "We're a melting pot of immigrants, hardworking citizens and a bastion of democracy."

Kiltman University professor of music Thomas Robert Fansler wrote the following sample lyrics that could replace the traditional ones. "They shouldn't be offensive," he said:

> Oh, say can you see,
> By each dawn's early light,
> What so proudly we hail,
> At each twilight's last gleaming?
> Whose broad stripes and bright stars,
> Through each challenging plight,
> O'er our cities it watches,
> while it's gallantly streaming.
> And from factories' red glare,
> The wheat waving in air
> There's proof that we're right,
> About the liberties we share.
> Oh say does that star spangled banner yet wave,
> O'er the land of the free, and the home of the brave.

Only time will tell whether the conservatives will try to block this change in our National Anthem or whether it will go the way of many amateur sports mascots and a host of Confederate statues.

ERSATZ VIEWS

NO MATTER WHO WON THE 2016 ELECTION THERE SHOULD HAVE BEEN RIOTING IN THE STREETS

By Samuel Goens

How ironic! We've been wanting a transparent president and now that we've got one we're appalled. Is this really what capitalist moguls are like? Yes, and he's open about it.

Is he like a lot of former presidents and statesmen? Yes, we know Jefferson slept with one of his slaves, Franklin had children but never married, Kennedy kept two "secretaries" on the White House staff just as playthings, FDR and Eisenhower both had mistresses.

I'm sure there are plenty of clandestine and immoral things we don't know. I had a friend who was privy to what's really going with our military and leaders. He told me: "I cannot give details. Well, now that I think about it, I probably could because you wouldn't believe the things we've done anyway."

We prefer our presidents to be slick, diplomatic, full of BS, promising the moon, quietly immoral, hegemonic and living like kings. I remember voting for Carter because he was honest, moral and practical. When we had an oil shortage and gas and oil prices rose, he told the nation to put on sweaters and he wore one too. He didn't say we should go to war to straighten this oil problem out. He didn't have as many lavish dinners to show off in the White House. He was one of us.

Boy, we got rid of him fast and elected Hollywood Reagan. Slick on the outside, lived like royalty and lied about what was going on in Nicaragua, which was breaking the law. His trickledown economics obviously was about some bodily fluid not money.

The popular vote in the last election went to Hillary, who probably lost the Electoral College because she refused to be transparent. With the memory of what she had done and knowledge of what was going on under the table, plus memories of what her husband lied about going on under the desk, haunted her--altruistic on the outside and self-serving on the inside. The Clintons became millionaires in politics as our servants. Figure that out.

Some of Trumps actions are egotistical, shocking, immoral, poorly thought out, undiplomatic, etc. His error with the American people is being transparent. I've read dozens of books written during the last 150 years. The accusations in these books about the problems with the economy and government are the same in every decade: money, Wall Street, career politicians, corruption in Washington and large cities, over regulation, big government, lack of fiscal responsibility, riders, gerrymandering, obstructionism, ignoring the constitution, sexual misconduct, constant war, etc.

New faces appear in Washington once in a while, but nothing changes for the better. The rich get richer and the rest get promises. When I say I voted for Perot and Sanders, people laugh. When they tell me who they voted for, I just shake my head. Americans want to be in a perpetual Disneyland, but is a dismal land instead?

One More Nickname

Ersatz News—'It lives up to its name'

After months of campaigning, debates, the election and Donald Trump taking office, the nation finally discovers President Trump's nickname for himself. Most of last year the debates and news analysis was full of the following:

Truly Weird Rand Paul

Crazy Bernie

Goofy Elizabeth Warren

Lyin' Ted

Crooked Hillary

Low-Energy Jeb

Little Marco

Nut Job Comey

Those who watched the O. J. Simpson criminal trial watched a Johnny Cochran repeat: "If the glove doesn't fit, you must acquit," and "If you can't trust the messenger, you can't trust the message." His repeating these and similar catchy phrases some said duped the jury into finding Simpson not guilty.

Of course, when Simpson faced the civil trial later, he was found guilty. The world learned that if you repeat something often enough, even if it doesn't make sense, sane and reasonable people might begin to believe it.

Although many news anchors and talking heads reported on how sophomoric Trump's name calling was, they had to admit it seemed to work with a large group of registered voters and kept Trump's opponents on the defensive.

A pre-election Trump ex-staff member that wants to remain anonymous overheard one campaign adviser playfully ask her boss what nickname he would use for himself if he had been his opponent. She said he laughed and said, "Donald the Twit."

The ex-staffer was surprised he would make that known and asked him about the affect if that got around. She said he grinned and said that it won't get any coverage because the media is on their heels and spending all their time defending themselves from being called the enemy of the American people and purveyors of fake news.

Making the Kall, by Howard Kall
Ersatz Views—'We live up to our name.'

A Kick in the Butt

Students don't learn because they get too few kicks in the butt. Plus, they outnumber teachers and parents. Plus, they have lawyers on their sides. Plus, there is a whole group of people who have never gotten their pets or children under control and think that a firm pat on the butt is child abuse.

Children used to learn to be master craftsmen by working as apprentices. They had to work alongside adults, doing the menial work, until they had enough knowledge, responsibility, skill and experience to do master-level work.

If apprentices goofed off, came in late or performed sloppy work, they got a firm kick in the butt the first time. If they continued in the same vein, they were tossed out on the street to find another job. When they went home the parents also gave them a good kick in the butt.

Today, if students goof off, come in late, skip school and do sloppy work, they can still earn a diploma. Seventy percent efficiency is acceptable to pass a grade. Schools also use the 1-2-3 method of discipline. We've seen that work in public places with children, right!

The 1-2-3 method is for people who don't want to take action against bad behavior. Kids can get two tardies to any class before getting detention. That's from 10 to 12 tardies when you consider they take five or six classes. Since most teachers also don't want to go through the hassle involved with confrontation, the third infraction is often delayed or completely ignored.

I've seen parents do the same thing.

"I'm going to count to three. Okay. One."
No response.
"Two."
No response.
"Three."
No response.
"Okay, you're going to be in real trouble, buddy, if you don't behave right now. Straighten up."
 No response.
I like the "one" method. You tell students the rule and the consequences and then when they break it the first time they suffer the consequences. Schools now have all kinds of 1-2-3 programs. If students are trouble in the classroom, schools have in–suspensions, out-of-school suspensions, Saturday schools, summer schools, and alternative schools. How about parents and teachers just working on the behavior and keeping kids in the classroom. Let's bring back the One Rule.

Ersatz Educational News—'We live up to our name'

Hate the Classroom? Become an Administrator

Can't stand kids? Hate being cooped up in a cement block room with a bunch of students each day? Don't like exploring new subjects, grading papers and preparing lessons?

Then get out of the classroom and into a cushy office. Use an assistant principal, counselors and deans of students to handle parents, student discipline and other school problems. Hire a couple of secretaries to take your calls, write your memos and otherwise run interference so that you don't have to directly deal with students anymore than possible.

Why don't schools teach kids as much as they could? Because they are often run by people who don't really like teaching. They got their degrees in education, tried the classroom and then bailed out as soon as possible. Many still hate doing observations in classrooms because they find learning boring.

Worse, though, is that many principals come from the ranks of physical education teachers who took jobs in education because they wanted to be coaches. When they discovered that they weren't good coaches and disliked the classroom the two alternatives were prepare for another profession or find a new position in education. Find a new position in school was the easiest route.

Teachers of academic subjects especially realize with this type of administrator that sports in the school is far more important than what's going on in the classroom. Schools need administrators who miss the classroom, who work with teachers in the classroom on projects, who help prepare curriculum, and who love observing students discovering and growing through excellent lessons.

Entrepreneur Embarrasses Local Employers

ERSATZ NEWS FROM THE CAPITAL—
'we live up to our name'

A year ago entrepreneur John Sheets opened a technology assistant shop on Dunton's main street. Nothing new about a shop that provides a service not offered anyplace in town. That's usually welcomed by fellow business owners.

The shop has done a good business because thousands of people have been looking at their smart phones, laptops, tablets, audio assistants and basketful of remotes as something from outer space.

"We look at ourselves as technology 'plumbers,' so we'll go to the house and troubleshoot and train for a flat service fee, about the same as a plumber or a heating and air serviceman," says Sheets. "We also train or work with individuals in our shop for a fee."

Then why are many local business owners mad at him? Every worker, from maintenance man, techy, secretary, receptionist and Sheets himself earn the same base salary.

Troubleshooter, Inc. pays a base of $45,000 a year, then there are raises for degrees, certificates, experience, responsibility, etc. just as in any company. The base is about 3 times minimum wage.

No one has shorten hours to reduce mandatory state and government benefits.

"Don't use my name, but I bet Sheets is taking home more than his employees," states another Main Street businessman.

When asked about that, Sheets said, "If we take in more than overhead, repairs and salaries, sure I make more, but some months I make less than my employees.

"I know some employers will do everything they can to cut cost, which is good business. But I get a little upset when I see an employer in a million dollar house with two $60,000 cars, an expensive boat, snowmobile, motorcycle and cottage on the lake while the people making him money only get minimum wage, no benefits and few hours. That's not the American way."

An employee at a local hardware complained that her employer is constantly refusing to increase pay while telling everyone how the construction of his second home in Florida is progressing. "At employee meetings he explains sales are down and profit are too," she stated. "We're not stupid. It makes us angry. It does not make me want to work very hard for him."

Thousands of Americans Return to their Homelands

ERSATZ NEWS: Chicago 'we live up to our name'

A new trend has scores of American citizens seeking out ancestral ties and endeavoring to learn more about their forebears' homelands.

The recent ease with which humans can have their DNA examined has helped Americans identify their great grandparents' countries of origin. In turn this has sparked an interest in research about and even travel to those countries.

"Although my name is Nelson, I found through a genealogical website that most of my ancestors were from Italy," says Wendy Nelson Applegate, of Carmel, Indiana. "I feel I know nothing about my heritage or that part of the world where my family came from. I'm planning my next vacation to the Perugia region of Umbria in Italy. That's where the Rubinos, Espositios and Sorrentinos lived. What an enticing mystery this all is for me."

"There's an inherent guilt about leaving your homeland and giving up your heritage," says psychologist Coy Dawkins. "Plus, many families beg those talking about immigrating to America to stay in the native country so there's not a 'brain drain' or loss of young people needed to support the family, community and country in the future."

Genealogist and historian Adam Graff says, "It's apparent that a feeling of 'homesickness' doesn't go away despite several generations living in America—there's a sense of emptiness that only searching out one's heritage can fill. It's kind of like adults who were adopted as children trying to discover who they are by finding their parents and the place where they were born. They want to fill the blank lines of their tribal slate."

Studies show that for Americans Great Britain, Germany, Ireland, Italy and France are the top locations for Americans wanting to immigrate. Not surprisingly, those are the same locations that are most popular for American travelers.

"Almost all Americans are immigrants, and some have a close tie to an ethnic community even after years here," says Serena Kole. "I remember my Polish grandmother wanted to go back to Poland, but she never had the money. She talked about missing walking in the mountains, tending sheep, living a simple life in a wonderful, small, friendly, picturesque village."

Kole went on to explain that her great grandfather was so poor he couldn't support his children, especially the girls, and arranging a marriage for women was hard because so many men had been lost in several wars involving Poland. So her grandmother was sent to live in a crowded apartment with her aunt and uncle in Chicago.

Like Kole's grandmother, many immigrants to America never completely feel that America is home, but they can't go back either.

Dawkins adds, "Those who come to America to live might be almost categorizes as 'people without a country.' That's why American cities continue to have China towns, Mexican barrios, Jewish neighborhoods, areas called Little Italy, and ethnic sections for Polish, Cubans, Haitians, Muslim and Blacks. There are also Swiss Amish and Dutch Mennonite and Scandinavian communities around the country. Ironically, Americans whose ancestors were immigrants don't always welcome new immigrants. It's like a 'I've got mine but I don't want you to get yours' attitude.

Sadly, after a while immigrants feel more at home here but less at home if they get a chance to return to Europe."

Still, thousands of second-, third- and fourth-generation Americans are returning to 'the old country' to live and refind their culture and continue with their ancestors' heritage.

Conservationists Call for Eradication of Non-Indigenous Species

ERSATZ NEWS—'we live up to our name'

National Environmental Coalition, National Parks, State Parks and state and national departments of natural resources are in a constant battle with invasive species.

Barbara Owens, NEC director, says, "Millions of dollars and thousands of hours by government employees and volunteers are put forth each year cutting down invasive plants, removing non-native animals, restoring natural habitats and reintroducing native species."

She went on to say that the destruction of habitat, loss of native fauna to predation by invaders, and the "upsetting of the balance of America's many orginal ecosystems is a national tragedy."

Research shows that the federal government has lacked the heart to take on the most serious problems because of public opinion. "Few people believe in real conservation, just like those worried about global warming continuing to drive gasoline engine cars and over cool and heat their houses," added Owens. "They send a check for $50 to a wildlife fund and their consciences are clear."

"Elected officials avoid the environmental concerns because they are more interested in votes than conservation," says the head of a Tennessee State Park. "When NEC calls for a congressional bill to start decreasing the numbers of the most prevalent nonindigenous animals--cows, hogs, chickens and sheep--the meat industry, restaurants and consumers forget about ecological concerns."

Owens says, "We know it's an uphill battle, but we've got to switch over to native meats at some point or our native habitats will never return. America will just be a mess of native species being crowed out by species with no predators to keep them in balance. Burmese pythons in Florida and kudzu in Georgia are good examples."

Historian Samuel Clouse stated: "We've already crowded out or marginalized the Native Americans, do we want to do that with North American flora and fauna too?"

North American mammals that could be domesticated for meat are several species of deer, antelope, American bison, elk, moose, caribou, bear, mountain goats, dahl sheep, rabbits, and smaller animals. Clouse says that "attempts to raise some of the native animals for meat have been initiated, but even with all of the fencing farmers and ranchers have done to make that easier, none has made a dent in the meat producing industry. As immigrants, we didn't adapt very well to the meats of the New World that were popular with the peoples already living here."

Are Those 'Other' Ingredients Healthy?

ERSATZ NEWS and VIEWS—"it lives up to its name"

We've all been told that all of the "other" ingredients in our processed and packaged foods are harmful. The Journal of Organic and Inorganic Compounds (JOIC) begs to differ.

The sulfites, sulfates, diphenyl, nisin, tiabendazol, formic acid, hexamethylenetetramine, formaldehyde, guaiac resin, boric acid, fumaric acid, uric acid, toluene, ammonium acetate, nitrites, nitrates, orthophenylphenol, and other ingredients found on processed food labels turn out to be good for humans and pets.

"Why are we surprised! The purpose of additives in processed food is preservation," says Sandi Gomes, head of research at Kensing Crown University in Toronto. "Whether you think this just makes sense or is ironic, doesn't matter, the health claims are true."

A recent KCU study proves that those minerals that increase the shelf life of fruits, meat and grains, also prolong the life of animals. As expected, those raising and marketing organic foods are saying that the claims are not true, the study is fake and the press releases are fake news.

Conserve Collect Communicate (CCC) director Hal Marsh says, "No way the JOIC article results are accurate! The chemical companies don't want their multi-billion dollar business in making and selling preservatives to disappear. I bet they sponsored the study if we could follow the money."

Of course, food manufacturers are silent for now, waiting to see if the claims hold up. After all, added chemicals make their products stay fresh longer, look more edible with added dyes, have more tang and/or exhibit more body. That they also have health benefits is great news.

JOIC claims that their publication is peer reviewed and those submitting articles must provide test documentation, annotations and sources along with the text. Experiments must meet US Scientific Standards.

Marsh adds, "These studies are not scientific. They just ask the elderly if they've been eating processed foods for 70 years or so and then write up the data. Well, it's probably more complicated than that, but I've seen studies where they test supplements by giving them to sufferers and then asking if they helped.

"The positive answers after a month are normally very high, maybe the placebo effect, but after a year most members of the trial will respond negatively. The real test is whether they buy the product on their own at the end of the program and take it for the rest of their life. About 7% do, but the rest find that there were no long-term health benefits. But the one-month studies are published and spread wholesale by talk show hosts on daytime television."

Get Out of the Educational "Snake Oil" Business

Helen Waybright, Ersatz News Education Columnist

I can think of few things that waste teachers' time and school funds more than "new" teaching techniques, strategies and initiatives. People who for some reason didn't want to continue teaching students in the classroom often come up with WOW, BAM, SNAP, CRACKLE and POP to make a living.

The programs often utilize acronyms, such as POP (Pupils On Point or something like that), to make some old idea sound new. Jargon works too. "Collaborative and holistic methodologies for integration of performance-based modular benchmark assessment." If there were such a program, it would probably mean teachers test kids to see if they know anything.

POP 'Pupils on Point'

Administrators often embrace these "new" programs thanks to a colleague, because jargon makes those out of the loop feel inferior–"You're not using POP!" The state of Indiana even initiated a multi-year project to help parents, teachers and administrators, entire communities, set goals for their schools. Tons of money and untold hours were spent in each community.

Most schools decided to focus on two goals. They sounded like these: math computation and reading comprehension, writing across the curriculum and problem solving, or daily journaling and intensified calculating.

The 3 Rs by any other Name

In other words, these educators while approaching the 21st Century discovered that schools should be teaching reading, writing and arithmetic–*the 3 R's*. Now that deserves a WOW(Waste of Worktime)!

Expensive educational snake oil claims, just like modern claims on infomercials, have promised to cure educational woes and make students angels and scholars for more than 100 years. And educators keep being lured in by the same empty promises under new hyped-up names.

Pop Fizzles

Sorry, teachers know, but keep hoping, that there's an easy answer. There's not. Schools need to get out of the snake-oil-buying business. To mix a few metaphors, the snap, crackle and pop of an old program dressed in new clothes turns out to be a big FIZZLE after a couple of years and is dropped.

AmericanAnti-Sexual-Harassment Solidarity

ERSATZ NEWS—'It lives up to its name.'

A surprising and selfless move by women in lofty and public positions has taken the male sexual harassment issue in a new direction.

At least a dozen women, according to a source, are going to come out and reveal that they were hired, not solely because of their extensive education and talent, but because they employed their sexual attractiveness. They worked hard all through high school and college to gain employment skills and then felt they had to stoop to using their looks as a key to success.

The source went on to explain that these women will apologize for utilizing short skirts, low necklines, makeup, plastic surgery, bare arms, brightly colored clothing and flirtatious gestures to be alluring to male and/or female employers.

Women in front of the camera—cable news anchors, weather girls, TV and screen actresses, professional cheerleaders and fashion models—are apparently among those who will speak out about how embarrassed they were using their sexuality to acquire and keep jobs, sometimes beating out their industry's female colleagues who had more education, experience and talent.

There apparently will be complaints of having to dye or bleach their hair, apply thick makeup and wear skimpy clothing while reading the news, whereas the men can be fat, have gray hair, wear white shirts and black suits that completely cover arms and legs. Actresses are asked to go further, often to expose their breasts or pose naked in a film, not to mention the 'director's couch.' "Sadly," added the source, "they often say yes to these demeaning requests."

The group wants to offer solidarity, support, empathy and encouragement, added the source, for those who have suffered under predatory and unpleasant gender treatment in the workplace.

Television journalist Makaya Canali, who claims not to be one of the group, said, "Sexual harassment is abhorrent, but I understand why these women are doing this. The problem, as I think they perceive it, is when women play the sex card to get employed, it opens our whole gender to a host of unexpected outcomes, not all pleasant. We become partially responsible for the whole problem of men's attitudes about women.

"Advertising and beauty contests don't help with sexy young girls wearing almost nothing. What are men, and women, to think, especially when they hear a thousand times something like 'every kiss begins with...a piece of jewelry.'

"It's shameful that some women and many companies enable men's inappropriate attitudes and behavior toward women, who they treat like cute, fancy toys. Often women use all the tricks in the book to turn men on and then act surprised or outraged when they work. Psychologist Eric Berne said that a certain tone or action often determines the reaction. So if a woman enters the workplace in a brightly colored above-the-knees dress, high heels, lots of makeup, a low-cut blouse displaying cleavage, and the like, the reaction is likely different than if she walked in dressed in neutral colored slacks, a simple long-sleeved, collared blouse, low heels and subdued makeup. It would be outrageous if a man showed up to work in a bright red sleeveless shirt, skin tight slacks, oiled muscles, chest hair showing, and anything else that would emphasize his manliness, physique and sexuality."

Feminist journalist Sandra Jones says, "Every time an escort or prostitute takes money from a man, every time a secretary sleeps with a boss, every time a woman tells her male friend or husband 'you're going to get lucky tonight,' after he buys her something or takes her out for a special meal, every time mothers dress up their girls in cute, skimpy, sexy outfits and push them onto a stage, into cheerleading, into beauty pageants, onto the beach, out into public, into modeling, etc., we women take a step backward in our endeavor to gain equal rights and pay and, especially, respect as intelligent, educated and skilled individuals.

"If we don't want to encourage sexual harassment, then we have to stop using sex as currency to pay back for favors. In the 21st Century of developed countries, women should be above that."

When Canali was asked whether these ladies speaking out would change things, her response was, "Not a chance! Men are strongly enticed by visual images, so they love women who make themselves look sexy. Women want to look and dress sexier than other women at a social event. Plus even the most liberal and well-educated women often deny any responsibility for sexual advances, so they see no reason to alter their behavior."

It's a two-sided game and it's part of our culture and the gender power struggle. Both sides try to take advantage of this modern anomaly. With makeup sales in America alone more than $60,000,000,000 a year, I think cosmetic companies would double the number of psychologists they hire to protect their message that women are not attractive unless they buy their products."

News agencies are using all their research abilities to try to identify the women who will speak out, knowing that they must have photos and copy ready as soon as the story goes public. So reporters are guessing then preparing videos clips and print material on hundreds of potential famous, beautiful and sexy women.

"It never ends, it just gets worse," stated Canali.

Harpton Takes a Stand on Gun Control

<u>*New York--Ersatz News—'it lives up to its name'*</u>
The latest round of mass and serial killings has rekindled efforts by citizens around the country who are pushing for more stringent gun regulations.

GAM (Guns Are a Menace) is one such group in Harpton, New York, that called on the town fathers to ban semi-automatic rifles and handguns for citizens in the city limit.

Several national rifle and handgun organizations and magazine publishers were quick to come to the rescue of those in town who wanted to oppose the ban. According to one magazine publisher, "We wanted to nip any movement against gun rights in the bud."

The Harpton town hall meeting started with Head City Father Jason Langley reading the current city gun regulations: "It is unlawful to discharge any firearm (handgun, rifle, shotgun, flare gun or any other instrument loaded with powder and a projectile) within the city limits of Harpton, New York."

Then he followed by stating that more than 4,000 residents had signed a request for a regulation prohibiting the ownership of semi-automatic rifles and handguns by Harpton, New York, citizens. The reasons listed were:

1. Semi-automatic handguns and rifles are being regularly used to kill children and teachers in schools, audience members at concerts and nightclubs and the citizens at other public gatherings. We need to be proactive so that these tragedies do not happen here.

2. Semi-automatic weapons are not needed for homeowner protection when a double barreled shotgun would be sufficient.
3. Local hunters don't need weapons with clips full of ammunition.
4. We know if enacted, this regulation would be a drop in the bucket that is American towns, counties and states. But a movement has to start somewhere. We want America to draw a line, with the first segment right here in Harpton, New York.

Responses from the audience included:

Jaime Bates: "The Second Amendment guarantees me the write to own my rifles. Don't you people who signed the petition believe in the Constitution?"

Howie Silenger: "You conveniently did not provide us with the full text of the gun clause:"

'A well regulated Militia, being necessary to the security of a free State, the right of the people to keep and bear Arms, shall not be infringed.'

Silenger: "Does Harpton have a city militia, does Harpton need a militia, if so, how is it being well regulated and by whom? Our well-regulated militia is the National Guard, and we also have the reserves and a national standing military (Army, Navy, Marines, Airforce and Coast Guard), plus the FBI, US Marshals, and city, county and state police. These people don't just go buy a gun and start using it, they're highly trained, well regulated, you might say. Who is a threat to our maintaining a free state? Centuries have passed since America was an infant nation that must call on the citizenry to grab rifles and meet the British approaching the outskirts of town. The concern addressed in the second amendment no longer exists or is applicable."

Bates: "Yeah, but what if the military tries to take over the government. How would we resist? Think about a president, the Commander and Chief of the army, wanting to become a dictator! Think about it!"

Maya Leger: "What's the joke about not taking a knife to a gun fight? I don't think a semi-automatic rifle could stand up to tanks, drone rockets, whatever. Think about that!"

Guns Express John Perry: "We must remember that guns are not the problem. Regulating guns will not stop mass or serial violence in America. It's not the guns that are at fault, but the persons misusing them."

Rex Moffit: "Tell that to the person with a shattered femur who is surrounded by a dozen dead and wounded. Ask them if they would prefer the killer had only access to a knife rather than a semiautomatic rifle or handgun."

Leger: With a chuckle, "I suppose it isn't the bullet from a gun that kills but the blood spurting out of the heart."

Carey Johnson: "You can kill a lot of people with a knife, ball bat or car too. Will we ban those from Harpton?"

Jessica Neal: Since guns and cars are each objects that are part of 33,000 deaths per year, you may have an idea there. Cars are not intentionally used for suicides and murders to the extent that guns are. Guns, especially the semi-automatic variety, have been proven very efficient killing weapons. If they weren't the military would be swapping them out for Billy clubs and hunting knives."

Jeremy Watts: "You're a f—king idiot. You're probably a New York City tree hugger who has never been in a real forest or hunted."

Neal: "Well, you're a first-class a—hole, and I bet…."

Langley: "Excuse me, but let me step in right here. Let's respect people on both sides of this debate."

Dr. Janis Dade: "I'm a psychologist…"

Unknown: Shouted, "Yeah, we've heard that plenty of times."

Audience: laughter.

Dr. Dade: "…and when people show their emotions in a debate it usually indicates they are frustrated because the other side has facts and common sense points…"

Unknown: "Shut up!"

Dr. Dade: "Like that. When your argument is weak, you double down, bluff, get louder and resort to name calling. As in Hamlet, 'Me thinks thou doth protest too much,' indicating your knowledge of your own mental deficiency."

Unknown: "Shut up!"

Langley: "Please!"

NRAA Rep Ed Claussen: "I can't stress the Second Amendment too much. Simply put, 'the right of the people to keep and bear Arms, shall not be infringed.' That means shall not be taken away, removed, negated, breached, limited, restricted, period. If we give up any constitutional rights, then we open the gate for government to continue to erode our freedoms. Let one go and eventually they're all gone. Americans will not stand for that, they never have stood for that and I'm sure real Americans in Harpton will not tolerate it."

High School Principal Jim Jones: "With all due respect Mr. Claussen, you're not part of the Harpton community and have only been in town one day. I don't think you know our beliefs as people who support America."

Unknown: "Hear. Hear."

Jones: "Secondly, I don't like debater's tricks. We get enough of the slippery slope fear tactics from media, shock jocks, emailers and social media material that assures us that 'the sky is falling' and the world is coming to an end because of this politician or that law or some Bible passage. I'm 55 and I've had to ignore a lot of predictions that we're on a slippery slope to hades. So, please Mr. Jones, don't think since Harpton is not New York City or Los Angeles that our citizens are dumb, backward or naive. And lastly, I don't like your use of begging the question, a logical fallacy, and the either/or fallacy. In this case you imply that citizens of Harpton can't be both real Americans and supporters of safe and reasonable gun regulations."

Hank Farrell: "I don't like changing laws. That represents loss of freedoms that we've had for decades. I also don't like the hand grenade method of solving a problem. Let's be more surgical, focusing on only those few who should not be allowed to have firearms and on current gun laws that aren't enforced, instead of interfering in the rights of thousands of us lawful, careful and responsible gun owners."

Jenny Cook: "I don't think any of us has ever seen a gun drawn and fired at someone unless we were in the military. Even then most soldiers don't see that either. My deceased husband's military service was spent in a motor pool on an Army base in California. He was a brave man, but he didn't see the horrors of gun wounds and death. My fear is that we'll send our kids to a college, a concert, a ball game or other event and then learn that some wacko has opened fire on them with an automatic weapon. I guess I mean semi-automatic weapon. Sometimes I'm afraid to go to an airport or mall. Why does any civilian need a weapon like this?"

Hank Sands: "I know why! Shorty over there can't hit the broad side of a barn with a shotgun. If he didn't have a semi-automatic to spray around in the woods, he'd never get his yearly buck for the Thanksgiving table."

Audience: Laughter.

Sara Wilson: "Larry, newspaper articles say you served bravely in combat. You shot and killed the enemy and were shot at in return. You're military, what do you think? You know about guns."

Larry Calhoun: "I really don't want to talk about my combat experiences, plus they have no bearing on the focus of this meeting. For the record, though, I don't own or need a weapon in Harpton."

Shadonna Abrams: "I notice the gun crowd from out of town has gotten quiet. Good. When I look at them I think of the motto of investigative reporters, 'Follow the money.' I'm sorry, but I have trouble taking the word of people who reap millions supporting a president, a gun lobby, a conservation group, some charities, or other groups with economic interests. I want to add to a point made by Principal Jones. People and companies who encourage paranoia through their ads, editorials, magazines, cable news and radio shows are seeking power and making tons of money stirring up anger and fear with questionable scenarios. That's how they get and keep their audience. Pure emotions but little common sense."

At this point the head of the town fathers let it be known that the fathers had an impression about how both side felt, and that now he would only allow facts, data and their sources. So Langley read:

> *Compared to 22 other high-income nations, the United States' gun-related murder rate is 25 times higher. And, even though the United States' suicide rate is similar to other countries, the nation's gun-related suicide rate is*

eight times higher than other high-income countries, researchers said.

> *--The study was published online Feb. 1, 2016, in The American Journal of Medicine. Reported on **CBS News**.*

A shooting at a California school, killing 5 and wounding 2, marks the 317th mass shooting in the U.S. so far this year.
According to data from the Gun Violence Archive, a total of 316 mass shooting incidents have occurred as of November 14, 2017. With the addition of Tuesday's school shooting, the total reaches 317.
Comparatively, 2016 saw a total of 483 mass shootings.

> *--Reported on **ABC News***

Assault rifles are becoming mass shooter's weapon of choice
Last night in Orlando, a man armed with an assault-style rifle killed at least 50 people and wounded 53 others in a crowded nightclub.

Six months ago, in San Bernardino, Calif., a man and woman armed with assault-style rifles killed 14 people and wounded 20 others at a holiday party.

In 2012, in Aurora, Colo., a man armed with an assault-style rifle killed 12 people and wounded 58 others in a crowded movie theater.

Also in 2012, in Newtown Conn., a man armed with an assault-style rifle killed 28 people and wounded 2 others at an elementary school

One common denominator behind these and other high-casualty mass shootings in recent years is the use of assault style rifles, capable of firing many rounds of ammunition in a relatively short period of time, with high accuracy. And their use in these types of shooting is becoming more common: There have been eight high-profile public mass shootings since July of last year, according to a database compiled by Mother

Jones magazine. Assault-style rifles were used in seven of those.
  --Reported in the **Washington Post**, June 12, 2016

Total for Gun Rights: $7,853,959
Total for Gun Control: $1,392,415
All lobbying expenditures on this page come from the Senate Office of Public Records. Data for the most recent year was downloaded on October 21, 2017.
  --Reported by **Opensecrets.org, Center for Responsive Politics**

What's wrong with the argument: Guns don't kill, people do?
I can't find a solid consensus regarding what exactly is wrong with it. Some think it begs the question, others think it equivocates, still others think it merely oversimplifies the issue. Consequently, especially as a logician, I think, "Guns don't kill people; people kill people," is an attempt to end a discussion about gun control, so point out that they have "mistaken the relevance of proximate causation.
  --Abstract from **Psychology Today**, February 12, 2013, David Kyle Johnson, Phd.

The Gun Rights representatives then handed out pamphlets and magazine articles from their publications.

QUIPS

Quips aimed at the dictators and citizens of the countries where I've lived or visited:
- Your country, just as in America, makes its own propaganda; just make sure you don't believe it.
- You don't have to drink hot tea in the summer if you keep your well water clean all year round.
- The longer dictators live the dumber they get and the angrier their people become.
- If police are paid enough they catch thieves instead of becoming thieves.
- Freedom of speech (media) helps keep politicians honest.
- Expensive walls hide poverty but don't help eliminate it.
- Showing off with spectacular events impresses everyday citizens but it doesn't improve their welfare.
- As rulers get rich, they forget the poor.
- Only poor students need tutors unless the teachers are poor.

For Americans and others in general:
- All writing is fiction; it's just mislabeled biography, journalism, history and truth.
- We Americans are at war, with the auto makers. We sacrifice 30,000 citizens a year on their altar. Of course, we have about the same number of gun deaths.
- Either/or Fallacy: There's a lot of grey matter between black and white.
- With a high school teen/teacher ratios of 30 to one, who do you think is actually in control?
- If you're not an imperialist or hegemonic nation, you don't have to have a large military stationed around the world.

- Tweet, media and Facebook discussions often disregard, excuse or hide the truth and common sense using red herring, post hoc ergo propter hoc, non sequitur, begging the question, ad hominem, slippery slope, composition/division, equivocation, and other logical fallacies. And few call the perpetrators out for it. Is this the new and acceptable "America Dialogue?" God help us!

About the Authors

Plenipoteniary Joel "Hubreesus" Robbins is an arhat polymath who, with all humility, is the self-proclaimed omniscient eremite sage living in a cloistered ashram high on a crag above the remote village of Nokomis.

Polyglot Mason Werner Robbins is an avid velocipede iconoclast that is a nascent scholar of middle school arithmetic and alternative antiquity. He is wed to a kenspeckle Caribbean *madame*, has two beautiful mulatto rapscallions, lives in Venice and owns a metaphysical sanctuary in the highlands of Hispaniola.

Other books by these authors are:

>InGear: Peace Corps and Beyond
>The Three Goals
>Ursa Caucasia
>Welsh Pears
>Appalachian Tales

Made in the USA
Monee, IL
03 January 2025